Classic
recipes

KT-415-777

over 60 recipes LOW IN POINTS

SIMON & SCHUSTER
A VIACOM COMPANY

Sue Ashworth

First published in Great Britain by Simon & Schuster UK Ltd, 2002.
A Viacom Company.

Copyright © 2002, Weight Watchers International, Inc.

Simon & Schuster UK Ltd.
Africa House
64–78 Kingsway
London WC2B 6AH

Weight Watchers and *Pure Points* are Trademarks
of Weight Watchers International, Inc. and used under its
control by Weight Watchers (UK) Ltd.

Photography: Iain Bagwell
Styling: Rachel Jukes
Food preparation: Penny Stephens
Design: Jane Humphrey
Typesetting: Stylize Digital Artwork
Printed in Hong Kong

Weight Watchers Publications Manager: Corrina Griffin
Weight Watchers Publications Executive: Lucy Davidson
Weight Watchers Publications Assistant: Celia Whiston

A CIP catalogue record for this book is available
from the British Library

ISBN 0 743 22056 0

Pictured on the front cover: Steak and Kidney Pie, page 36
Pictured on the back cover: Summer Pudding, page 52
Pictured on the title page: Sticky Banana Toffee Pudding, page 59

Raw Eggs

Only the freshest eggs should be used. Pregnant women, the elderly and children
should avoid recipes with eggs which are not fully cooked or raw. The Chocolate
Mousse with Raspberries (page 58) and Celebration Cake (page 63) contain raw eggs.

V denotes a vegetarian recipe and assumes vegetarian cheese and
free-range eggs are used. Virtually fat-free fromage frais and
low-fat crème fraîche may contain traces of gelatine so they are
not always vegetarian: please check the labels.

Vg denotes a vegan dish.

contents

favourite
recipes for
fewer points

Congratulations! By buying Weight Watchers Classic Recipes you are set to make small but significant changes to some of your everyday favourites. With the help of this book, you'll be able to give great-tasting basics the Weight Watchers treatment – making your mealtimes into healthy and nutritious options.

It's wonderful to try out new recipes – they liven up our eating patterns and add motivation, helping in our efforts to lose weight. Yet we all love the old favourites too – they're comforting, reliable and downright tasty. So that's what Classic Recipes is all about. It gives you the know-how to create the family's best-loved recipes in an easy-to-follow fashion – with the Weight Watchers touch to keep you on track.

Anyone who has followed the Weight Watchers *pure points*™ Programme will know just how easy and flexible dieting can be: no banned foods, no harsh rules and no regulations to make you feel like you're in a dieting straitjacket. Just freedom, flexibility and pure common sense that add up to one thing – results – which means that you are happier with the way you look and the way you feel. Weight Watchers can be a life-changing experience!

Let this cookbook be a back up to your plans to lose weight. For instance, when you want to cook a tasty Shepherd's Pie (page 40) or Toad-in-the-Hole (page 35) – check out our recipes first before following your usual method. Or if it's something fishy you're after, try our Traditional Fish Pie (page 16) or tuck into the Tuna Pasta Bake (page 20). The overall aim has been to reduce fat and calories in these recipes to keep the points lower. Yet it has been of paramount importance to keep the taste. When all is said and done, who's going to eat food that's bland and boring? Not any Weight Watchers Member in their right mind, that's for sure!

This book has six chapters full of mouth-watering recipes, so that you can plan a whole menu if you wish. There are tasty ideas for starters, soups and salads, and chapters on fish, chicken and meat. The vegetarian chapter is full of favourites – from Macaroni Cheese (page 49) to colourful Vegetable Curry (page 46). And don't ignore the meat and chicken sections if you are vegetarian – as we give several suggestions for vegetarian options. Looking for something luscious? The book wouldn't be complete without a section on desserts and cakes – a truly indulgent chapter with a healthy twist.

We hope that Classic Recipes will be a really useful addition to your cookbook collection. By increasing the amount of vegetables or fruit in recipes and reducing the ingredients that have higher fat contents, it has been possible to give you leaner, trimmer versions of your favourite recipes. This means that they are more healthy and nutritious too – giving your body all it needs for tip-top performance. So dip into this handy cookbook whenever you fancy a new favourite – and we promise it will go down a treat.

Sue Ashworth.

starters
soups & salads

The recipes in this chapter will get any meal off to a flying start. There are some delicious ideas for comforting soups, so when you fancy a bowlful of something warming, try them! And when you want a cool and crisp salad, there are plenty to choose from.

Whether you want something tasty for a starter or you're looking for ideas for a light meal, these recipes are the solution.

PRAWN COCKTAIL

POINTS	
per recipe: 8	per serving: 2

Serves: 4
Preparation time: 10 minutes
Freezing: not recommended
Calories per serving: 120

Year in, year out, prawn cocktail ranks as one of our all-time favourite starters – probably because it tastes so good!

6 tablespoons plain low-fat yogurt
2 tablespoons tomato ketchup
1 tablespoon tartare sauce
350 g (12 oz) cooked, peeled prawns, defrosted if frozen
1 bag of herb salad
1–2 teaspoons seasoned rice vinegar dressing or white wine vinegar
salt and freshly ground black pepper

TO GARNISH
1 tablespoon chopped fresh parsley (optional)
1 lime or lemon, sliced into wedges

1 In a medium bowl, mix together the yogurt, tomato ketchup and tartare sauce. Add the prawns and stir gently to coat. Season with salt and pepper.
2 Toss the salad leaves in the seasoned vinegar dressing or white wine vinegar, and then arrange on serving plates. Alternatively, shred the leaves and divide them between four attractive glasses.
3 Top the salad leaves with the prawn mixture. Garnish with chopped parsley, if using, and lime or lemon wedges, and serve.

TOP TIP You can buy Mitsukan Seasoned Rice Vinegar Dressing from most supermarkets and delicatessens. One tablespoon has just ½ a point, adding flavour and piquancy to salad leaves, so it's well worth looking out for.

VARIATION For a spicier version, stir ½ teaspoon of de-seeded, finely chopped fresh green chilli and a tablespoon of chopped fresh coriander into the prawn mixture, omitting the parsley. The points will remain the same.

**Prawn Cocktail:
Enjoy delicious
prawns in this
classic sauce for
only 2 points per
serving.**

**Garlic Mushrooms:
A fantastic 2½ point
snack or starter for
mushroom lovers.**

GARLIC MUSHROOMS

POINTS

per recipe: 5	per serving: 2½

Ⓥ *if using vegetarian cheese*

Serves: 2

Preparation time: 10 minutes

Cooking time: 15 minutes

Freezing: not recommended

Calories per serving: 115

Serve one mushroom each for a starter. For a light meal, serve two per person and accompany with steamed carrots, courgettes and broccoli instead of the lettuce and tomato.

2 very large flat mushrooms, wiped

low-fat cooking spray

2 spring onions, trimmed and finely chopped

125 g (4½ oz) tub of low-fat soft cheese with garlic and herbs

1 tablespoon fresh white breadcrumbs

1 tablespoon finely grated Parmesan cheese

salt and freshly ground black pepper

chopped fresh parsley, to garnish

TO SERVE

shredded lettuce

cherry tomatoes

1 Preheat the oven to Gas Mark 6/ 200°C/400°F.

2 Remove the stalks from the mushrooms and finely chop them. Spray a frying pan three times with the low-fat cooking spray. Heat the pan, add the mushroom stalks and spring onions and cook them until softened – about 3 minutes. Cool slightly.

3 Meanwhile, spray each side of the mushroom caps with low-fat cooking spray and put them in a baking dish, with the brown gills facing upwards. Mix the soft cheese with the spring onion mixture and use it to fill the mushroom caps. Season with salt and pepper.

4 Mix the breadcrumbs and Parmesan cheese together and sprinkle the mixture over the mushrooms. Bake for 10–12 minutes until cooked.

5 Garnish the mushrooms with chopped fresh parsley, and serve with shredded lettuce and cherry tomatoes.

TOP TIP If you can't find low-fat soft cheese with garlic and herbs, just use the plain variety and add a crushed garlic clove to the frying pan with the spring onions. Stir a tablespoon of chopped fresh parsley – or herbs of your choice – into the mixture before filling the mushrooms. The points will remain the same.

LEEK AND POTATO SOUP

POINTS

per recipe: 8½	per serving: 1½

Ⓥ Serves: 6

Preparation time: 15 minutes

Cooking time: 35 minutes

Freezing: recommended

Calories per serving: 130

This soup is delicious, filling and so simple to make. It freezes well, so why not make plenty of it so you can eat some now and save the rest for later.

1 tablespoon polyunsaturated margarine

1 large onion, chopped finely

500 g (1lb 2 oz) leeks, chopped finely

500 g (1lb 2 oz) floury potatoes, peeled and chopped

3 tablespoons chopped fresh parsley, plus a few sprigs, to garnish

3 vegetable stock cubes, dissolved in 1 litre (1¾ pints) hot water

300 ml (½ pint) skimmed milk

salt and freshly ground black pepper

1 Melt the margarine in a large saucepan and gently sauté the onion and leeks until soft, about 10 minutes.

2 Add the potatoes, parsley and hot stock and bring to the boil. Cover and reduce the heat. Simmer gently for about 20 minutes, or until the vegetables are tender and the potatoes are beginning to break down.

3 Add the milk to the saucepan and reheat gently. Season to taste with salt and pepper and then ladle the soup into warmed bowls. Serve, garnished with parsley sprigs.

TOP TIP If you prefer, liquidise the soup in a blender or food processor to make it extra smooth.

VARIATION Just use onions instead of leeks if you like – the soup will still be delicious. The points will remain the same.

1 Melt the margarine in a large saucepan and gently sauté the onion, leek, celery and parsnip until softened, about 10 minutes.

2 Add the chicken to the saucepan with the hot stock. Bring to the boil and then reduce the heat. Cover and simmer gently for 30 minutes.

3 Using a draining spoon, lift the chicken from the saucepan and put it on a chopping board. Let it cool down for a few minutes and then use two forks to strip off all the meat. Discard the bones.

4 Transfer the soup to a blender or food processor and add half the chicken and all the fromage frais. Blend for about 15–20 seconds until smooth. Return the soup to the saucepan, add the parsley and remaining chicken and reheat gently.

5 Season to taste with salt and pepper, ladle into warmed soup bowls and serve at once.

TOP TIP Cooking the chicken portion in the stock gives the soup extra flavour.

Cream of Chicken Soup: Wonderfully warming – a timeless classic.

CREAM OF CHICKEN SOUP

POINTS

per recipe: 11   per serving: 3

V *if following variation*

Serves: 4

Preparation time: 10 minutes

Cooking time: 45 minutes

Freezing: recommended

Calories per serving: 130

Comforting and delicious, who can resist a piping hot bowlful of chicken soup? It will really lift your spirits.

1 tablespoon polyunsaturated margarine

1 onion, chopped finely

1 leek, sliced finely

3 celery sticks, chopped

1 medium parsnip, chopped

1 × 250 g (9 oz) medium chicken leg quarter, skinned

2 chicken or vegetable stock cubes, dissolved in 1.2 litres (2 pints) hot water

100 g (3¹/₂ oz) very low-fat plain fromage frais

2 tablespoons chopped fresh parsley

salt and freshly ground black pepper

VARIATION To make a cream of vegetable soup, omit the chicken and use vegetable stock cubes. Add a couple of chopped carrots to the saucepan and sauté them with the other vegetables. Points per serving will be 1.

QUICK TOMATO SOUP

POINTS	
per recipe: **2**	**per serving:** ½

Ⓥ *Serves: 4*
Preparation time: 10 minutes
Cooking time: 15 minutes
Freezing: recommended
Calories per serving: 90

Why not enjoy a bowl of this tasty soup before you go out for a special meal? It will curb your appetite, and reduce the temptation to eat too much later.

1 large onion, chopped

2 celery sticks, chopped

2 garlic cloves, crushed

2 vegetable stock cubes, dissolved in 450 ml (16 fl oz) hot water

2 × 400 g cans chopped tomatoes

2 tablespoons tomato purée

1 tablespoon dried mixed herbs

1 teaspoon dark or light muscovado sugar

1 tablespoon cornflour, blended with 3 tablespoons cold water

salt and freshly ground black pepper

4 tablespoons plain low-fat yogurt, to serve

celery leaves, to garnish (optional)

1 Put the onion, celery and garlic in a large saucepan and pour in the hot stock. Bring to the boil, and then reduce the heat. Simmer for 5 minutes.
2 Add the chopped tomatoes, tomato purée, dried herbs and muscovado sugar. Bring to the boil once more and then reduce the heat. Simmer for 5 minutes.

3 Transfer the soup to a blender or food processor and whizz together for about 15 seconds, until smooth.
4 Pour the soup back into the saucepan and stir in the blended cornflour. Reheat gently, stirring constantly until the soup thickens slightly. Cook for another minute or two. Season to taste. Serve each bowlful topped with a tablespoon of plain low-fat yogurt, a few celery leaves and a little more ground black pepper.

TOP TIP Try using economy canned whole plum tomatoes in this recipe – chop them roughly first. This only takes a few moments and it makes the recipe more economical.

VARIATION To make a cream of tomato soup, add a 200 g tub of low-fat soft cheese to the blender or food processor when liquidising. This will add a further 1½ points to each portion of soup.

Quick Tomato Soup: Enjoy a bowl for only ½ a point! Add 2½ points for 2 medium slices of bread.

Mulligatawny Soup: One of the all-time favourite soups.

MULLIGATAWNY SOUP

POINTS

per recipe: $4^{1}/_{2}$ per serving: 1

V   Serves: 4

Preparation time: 10 minutes
Cooking time: 25 minutes
Freezing: recommended
Calories per serving: 140

Hot, spicy and warming; this tasty soup is just the thing for a chilly day.

---

1 tablespoon vegetable oil

1 medium onion, chopped

1 medium eating apple, peeled and chopped

2 garlic cloves, crushed

1 medium parsnip, chopped

2 medium carrots, sliced

1 tablespoon medium curry powder

2 vegetable stock cubes, dissolved in 1 litre (1³/₄ pints) hot water

200 g can of chopped tomatoes

125 g (4¹/₂ oz) cauliflower, broken into small florets

125 g (4¹/₂ oz) fine green beans, sliced

2 tablespoons chopped fresh coriander, plus extra, for garnish

salt and freshly ground black pepper

4 tablespoons plain low-fat yogurt, to serve

---

1 Heat the vegetable oil in a very large saucepan and add the onion, apple and garlic. Sauté gently for 3–4 minutes and then add the parsnip, carrots and curry powder. Cook gently, stirring, for another minute.

2 Pour in the vegetable stock and tomatoes and bring up to the boil. Reduce the heat, cover and simmer gently for 10 minutes.

3 Add the cauliflower, green beans and coriander to the saucepan. Cover and simmer for a further 10 minutes, or until the vegetables are tender.

4 Season to taste, adding a little more curry powder if you wish. Top each bowlful with one tablespoon of yogurt and then serve, garnished with coriander.

TOP TIP If you prefer a smooth soup, liquidise the cooked mixture in a blender or food processor for about 15–20 seconds.

VARIATION Use a mild or hot curry powder instead of medium – according to your own preferences.

SEAFOOD CHOWDER

POINTS

per recipe: $13^{1}/_{2}$ per serving: $3^{1}/_{2}$

Serves: 4

Preparation time: 10 minutes
Cooking time: 20 minutes
Calories per serving: 255
Freezing: recommended

This delicious seafood soup is a meal in itself.

---

1 tablespoon vegetable oil

1 bunch spring onions, trimmed and chopped finely

2 fish or vegetable stock cubes, dissolved in 450 ml (16 fl oz) hot water

350 g (12 oz) smoked cod fillet

600 ml (1 pint) skimmed milk

50 g (1³/₄ oz) frozen peas

50 g (1³/₄ oz) frozen sweetcorn

125 g (4¹/₂ oz) frozen, peeled prawns, defrosted

2 tablespoons chopped fresh coriander or parsley, plus extra, to garnish

2 tablespoons cornflour, blended with 4 tablespoons cold water

salt and freshly ground black pepper

---

1 Heat the vegetable oil in a very large saucepan and sauté the spring onions for 2–3 minutes.

2 Pour in the stock and bring up to simmering point. Add the cod fillet. Turn the heat to low and simmer gently for 5–6 minutes. Lift out the fish with a draining spoon and flake it with a fork, discarding the skin and any bones.

3 Add the milk, peas, sweetcorn, prawns and coriander or parsley to the saucepan. Bring to the boil and then reduce the heat. Simmer for 3–4 minutes.

4 Stir the blended cornflour and add it to the saucepan. Bring to the boil, stirring until thickened.

5 Return the smoked cod to the saucepan. Cook gently for about 1 minute until heated through. Taste the soup and season it with salt and pepper. Ladle it into warmed soup bowls and add a little extra chopped coriander or parsley.

TUNA NIÇOISE

POINTS

per recipe: 12   per serving: 3

(v) *if following the variation*

Serves: 4

Preparation and cooking time: 25 minutes

Freezing: not recommended

Calories per serving: 245

Canned tuna fish is excellent in this great store-cupboard standby. Serve with a medium portion of boiled new potatoes (200 g/7 oz) for a meal, adding 2 points per serving.

175 g (6 oz) fine green beans

1/2 iceberg lettuce, shredded

4 small tomatoes, cut into wedges

1/2 small cucumber, sliced

1 bunch spring onions, trimmed and sliced

2 × 185 g cans tuna fish in brine, drained

4 medium eggs, hard-boiled and quartered

12 stoned black olives, sliced

1 tablespoon capers

2 tablespoons chopped fresh parsley (flat-leaf, preferably)

1 tablespoon olive oil

2 tablespoons lemon juice

1 teaspoon Dijon mustard

salt and freshly ground black pepper

1 Cook the green beans in lightly salted boiling water until just tender, about 5 minutes. Drain them well.

2 Divide the lettuce, tomatoes, cucumber, spring onions and green beans between four serving plates. Flake the tuna fish and share it out between the four portions.

3 Allow one egg per portion, and arrange the quarters on the salads. Scatter with the olives and capers. Sprinkle with the chopped parsley.

4 Mix together the olive oil, lemon juice and mustard. Season with salt and pepper. Use to dress the salads and serve at once.

TOP TIP If you're not keen on capers, simply leave them out.

VARIATION To make a vegetarian version, omit the tuna and use 75 g (2¾ oz) feta cheese instead. The points per serving will be 3½.

Tuna Nicoise: This delicious salad from the south of France is ideal as a light meal for only 3 points per serving.

CAESAR SALAD

POINTS

per recipe: 4½   per serving: 4½

Serves: 1

Preparation time: 15 minutes

Freezing: not recommended

Calories per serving: 190

Caesar salad is really delicious, with its crisp fresh lettuce, crunchy garlic croûtons and freshly grated Parmesan cheese.

2 anchovies in olive oil, rinsed

1 teaspoon olive oil

1 tablespoon plain low-fat yogurt

1/2 teaspoon Dijon mustard

a few Cos lettuce leaves, thoroughly washed

1 tablespoon finely grated Parmesan cheese

1 teaspoon low-fat spread

1 small garlic clove, crushed (or 1/2 teaspoon garlic purée)

1 × 25 g (1 oz) slice of white bread

salt and freshly ground black pepper

1 Pulverise the anchovies with a pestle and mortar until they form a paste. Whisk in the olive oil, yogurt and mustard. Season with salt and black pepper.

2 Roughly tear the lettuce into a salad bowl. Add the dressing and toss well. Sprinkle with the Parmesan.

3 Mix the low-fat spread and crushed garlic or garlic purée together. Toast the bread on one side and spread the other side with the garlic mixture. Grill until browned and then cut into cubes. Sprinkle over the salad. Serve at once.

VARIATION Caesar salad is delicious if you top it with some crispy-cooked chicken. Simply shred a 50 g (1¾ oz) cooked chicken breast and stir-fry it in 1 teaspoon of olive oil until browned and crispy. This will add 2 points per serving.

SMOKED FISH PÂTÉ

POINTS

per recipe: 4   per serving: 1

Serves: 4
Preparation and cooking time: 30 minutes
Freezing: not recommended
Calories per serving: 105

Serve this low-point fish pâté with a mixed salad for no extra points or with one medium slice of toast for 1 extra point.

400 g (14 oz) smoked haddock

1 bay leaf

4 tablespoons 0% fat plain Greek yogurt

1 tablespoon horseradish sauce

1 teaspoon wholegrain mustard

1 tablespoon chopped fresh parsley

1 tablespoon chopped fresh chives or spring onions

freshly ground black pepper

1–2 teaspoons lemon juice, according to taste

TO GARNISH

lemon slices

parsley or chives

1 Place the haddock in a shallow pan and cover with water. Add the bay leaf. Heat until just simmering and then cook gently for about 6–8 minutes, until the fish is cooked. The flesh should be opaque and flake easily when tested with a fork.

2 Lift the fish from the pan and let it cool down. Flake it with a fork, removing the skin and any bones. Put it into a bowl and mash thoroughly with a fork.

3 Add the yogurt, horseradish sauce, mustard, parsley and chives or spring onions to the fish. Season with black pepper and stir together to mix thoroughly. Taste, adding a little lemon juice, if needed. The pâté should be salty enough, but add a little extra salt if you wish.

4 Pack the pâté into individual dishes or ramekins, or put it into one large dish. Cover and refrigerate until ready to serve. Garnish with lemon slices and parsley or chives.

VARIATION This pâté is delicious when smoked mackerel is used instead of haddock. This fish is already cooked. You can buy the fillets from the deli section at your supermarket. Just remove the skin and any bones as before. If you use smoked mackerel, points will be higher because the fish is oily, working out to 7 points per portion. The solution – serve half as much at 3½ points each.

APPLE AND CELERY COLESLAW

POINTS

per recipe: 6½   per serving: 1½

 Serves: 4
Preparation time: 10 minutes
Freezing: not recommended
Calories per serving: 130

Traditional coleslaw can be quite high in fat and calories but this version reduces the points by using low-fat plain yogurt instead of mayonnaise.

2 tablespoons lemon juice

1 red apple, chopped

300 g (10½ oz) firm white cabbage, shredded

100 g (3½ oz) small red cabbage, shredded

1 medium carrot, grated

4 spring onions, sliced finely

3 celery sticks, sliced finely

50g (1¾ oz) sultanas or raisins

100 g (3½ oz) seedless red or green grapes, halved

300ml (½ pint) low-fat plain yogurt

salt and freshly ground black pepper

1 Put the lemon juice in a large mixing bowl and add the chopped apple tossing well to coat it, so that it doesn't turn brown.

2 Add all the remaining ingredients, stirring thoroughly to mix. Season to taste with salt and pepper.

VARIATIONS For extra crunch, add 2 tablespoons of lightly toasted sunflower seeds. This will add a ½ point to each serving.

Half a portion of this coleslaw tastes delicious on a ham sandwich made with two medium slices of white or brown bread and a medium portion 30 g (1¼ oz) of wafer-thin ham for 4½ points per serving.

Smoked Fish Pâté: The classic combination of pâté and toast for a total of only 2 points.

fish

Fish is an excellent food. It's very nutritious as it is low in fat, yet high in protein and minerals. Its point value is very low, meaning you can have a generous portion, so that you don't even feel like you're trying to lose weight.

TRADITIONAL FISH PIE

POINTS

per recipe: 22   per serving: 5½

Serves: 4
Preparation time: 20 minutes
Cooking time: 1 hour
Freezing: recommended
Calories per serving: 390

Fish pie is so delicious and it's a dish that all the family will enjoy. Serve with plenty of zero-point vegetables, such as carrots, broccoli or green beans.

700 g (1 lb 9 oz) potatoes, peeled

2 large leeks, chopped

300ml (½ pint) plus 2 tablespoons skimmed milk

1 tablespoon chopped fresh parsley or chives, plus extra, to garnish

25 g (1 oz) polyunsaturated margarine

50 g (1¾ oz) plain white flour

450 g (1 lb) skinned and boned cod, cut into chunks

100 g (3½ oz) frozen, peeled prawns, defrosted

50 g (1¾ oz) frozen peas, defrosted

salt and freshly ground black pepper

1 Cook the potatoes in boiling, lightly salted water until just tender. Meanwhile, cook the leeks in a small amount of lightly salted boiling water for about 5 minutes. Drain them both well, reserving the cooking liquid.

2 Mash the potatoes, adding 2 tablespoons of milk. Make the remaining 300 ml (½ pint) of milk up to 450 ml (16 fl oz) with the cooking liquid from the potatoes and leeks. Add the chopped parsley or chives.

3 Put the margarine, flour and milk mixture into a saucepan. Heat, stirring constantly with a small wire whisk or wooden spoon, until thickened and smooth. Check the seasoning, adding salt and pepper if necessary.

4 Preheat the oven to Gas Mark 5/ 190°C/375°F.

5 Put the cod in the base of a 1.2 litre (2-pint) baking dish and scatter the cooked leeks, prawns and peas on top. Pour over the sauce. Pipe or spoon the mashed potato over the surface.

6 Bake in the oven for 30–35 minutes until cooked and browned, then serve, sprinkled with more chopped parsley or chives.

Traditional Fish Pie: Everyone's favourite for only 5½ points.

Cod with Parsley Sauce: A quick, easy and delicious supper for one.

KEDGEREE

Serves: 4
Preparation time: 20 minutes
Cooking time: 25 minutes
Freezing: recommended
Calories per serving: 355

Although this recipe used to be a traditional breakfast dish, you'll find it makes a very tasty meal for lunch or supper.

450 g (1 lb) smoked cod or haddock fillets
1 vegetable stock cube
1 tablespoon olive or vegetable oil
175 g (6 oz) long-grain rice
1 medium onion, chopped
½ teaspoon cumin seeds
2 teaspoons medium curry powder
2 medium eggs, hard-boiled and quartered
2 tablespoons chopped fresh parsley, plus extra to garnish
salt and freshly ground black pepper

1 Put the fish fillets in a large frying pan and pour in enough cold water just to cover them. Poach gently for about 5 minutes, until the flesh looks opaque and flakes easily when tested with a fork.

2 Lift the fish from the frying pan, discard any skin and bones and then flake the flesh roughly. Strain the cooking liquid into a measuring jug and make it up to 850 ml (1½ pints) with hot water. Add the vegetable stock cube and let it dissolve.

3 Heat the oil in a frying pan and add the rice and onion. Sauté them gently for about 5 minutes. Add the cumin seeds and curry powder and cook for another 30 seconds or so.

4 Add the stock to the pan and bring to the boil. Reduce the heat and simmer, uncovered – stirring from time to time – until all the liquid has been absorbed and the rice is cooked. Add a little extra water if necessary.

5 Add the fish, hard-boiled eggs and parsley to the cooked rice, and stir through gently. Season with salt and pepper. Heat thoroughly for 2–3 minutes, garnish with fresh parsley and then serve.

VARIATION For an even tastier version of this delicious dish, use half salmon fillets and half smoked haddock or cod. Points per serving will be 5½.

COD WITH PARSLEY SAUCE

Serves: 1
Preparation time: 5 minutes
Cooking time: 20 minutes
Freezing: not recommended
Calories per serving: 245

A well-flavoured parsley sauce perfectly complements cod – or any white fish. Accompany this dish with fresh zero-point vegetables.

175 g (6 oz) cod fillet
1 bay leaf
50 ml (2 fl oz) skimmed milk
1 teaspoon polyunsaturated margarine
1 tablespoon plain white flour
1 tablespoon chopped fresh parsley, plus extra, to garnish
salt and freshly ground black pepper

1 Put the fish in a shallow pan and add just enough cold water to cover it. Add the bay leaf. Heat gently and poach the fish for about 6–8 minutes until cooked, when the flesh will be opaque and will flake easily.

2 Strain 50 ml (2 fl oz) of the fish cooking liquid into a saucepan. Cover the fish and keep it warm.

3 Add the milk, margarine and flour to the fish stock and heat it, stirring the mixture constantly with a small wire whisk until the sauce thickens. Remove from the heat and add the parsley. Season with salt and pepper.

4 Pour the sauce over the fish, garnish with chopped parsley and serve at once.

VARIATION For Cod Mornay, add 15 g (½ oz) of finely grated extra-mature Cheddar cheese to the hot sauce stirring it until melted (step 3). Adjust the points to 5½ per serving.

1 Preheat the oven to Gas Mark 5/ 190°C/375°F. Mist a 600 ml (1-pint) ovenproof dish with the low-fat cooking spray.

2 Cook the pasta shapes in lightly salted boiling water for about 10 minutes, or according to pack instructions, until tender. Drain well. While waiting for the pasta, cook the broccoli florets in lightly salted boiling water for about 6 minutes, until tender. Drain well.

3 Tip the pasta shapes, broccoli and flaked tuna into the prepared baking dish, distributing them evenly. Beat together the eggs, milk and parsley; season with salt and pepper. Pour into the dish and sprinkle the cheese over the top.

4 Bake for 35–40 minutes until set and golden. Serve with the salad and tomatoes.

TOP TIP Be sure to use a mature Cheddar for this recipe – because you are using less, you need the extra flavour.

Tuna Pasta Bake: A family classic for only 5 points per serving.

TUNA PASTA BAKE

POINTS

per recipe: 10	per serving: 5

Serves: 2
Preparation time: 20 minutes
Cooking time: 45–50 minutes
Freezing: recommended
Calories per serving: 360

This easy pasta bake is a great store-cupboard standby – and it's delicious too.

low-fat cooking spray

40 g (1½ oz) dried pasta shapes

100 g (3½ oz) broccoli, broken into florets

200 g can of tuna in brine or water, drained and flaked

2 small eggs

150 ml (¼ pint) skimmed milk

1 tablespoon chopped fresh parsley (or ½ teaspoon of dried)

25 g (1 oz) mature Cheddar cheese, grated

salt and freshly ground black pepper

TO SERVE

1 bag of mixed salad leaves

4 tomatoes

FABULOUS FISH CAKES

POINTS

per recipe: **21½**   per serving: **5½**

Serves: 4
Preparation time: 20 minutes
Cooking time: 30–35 minutes
Freezing: recommended
Calories per serving: 255

Serve with a packet of zero-point stir-fry vegetables, cooked in 1 tablespoon of stir-fry oil or vegetable oil for 3 to 4 minutes. Season with a few drops of soy sauce and chilli sauce adding ½ a point per serving.

225 g (8 oz) smoked haddock
225 g (8 oz) cod
450 g (1 lb) cold, mashed potato
4 spring onions, chopped finely
2 teaspoons Thai red or green curry paste (optional)
1 small egg, beaten
75 g (2¾ oz) frozen sweetcorn, defrosted
3 tablespoons plain white flour
salt and freshly ground black pepper
chives or spring onions, to garnish
a handful of mixed salad leaves, to serve

1 Put the fish fillets in a large frying pan and pour in enough cold water just to cover them. Poach gently for 5–6 minutes, until the flesh looks opaque and flakes easily when tested with a fork.

2 Lift the fish from the frying pan, discard any skin and bones and then flake the flesh roughly. Allow to cool completely.

3 Preheat the oven to Gas Mark 5/ 190°C/375°F. Put the potato in a large bowl and mix in the spring onions, red or green curry paste (if using), egg and sweetcorn. Add the fish, season with salt and pepper and mix together gently. Form the mixture into eight fish cakes and dust them with flour.

4 Place the fish cakes on baking sheets and bake them in the oven for 30–35 minutes, until brown.

5 Allow two fish cakes per person. Garnish with chives or spring onions and serve with some mixed salad leaves.

TOP TIP The Thai red or green curry paste gives the fish cakes an extra kick – though you can leave it out if you prefer, saving ½ a point per serving.

VARIATIONS Try using 3 tablespoons of polenta instead of flour for coating the fish cakes – it gives them a slightly crunchier finish. Points will be 5 per serving.

For a tasty shortcut, replace the fresh fish with canned tuna. Use 2 × 200 g cans of tuna in brine or water, thoroughly drained. This will reduce the points to 5 per serving.

Fabulous Fish Cakes: Only 5½ points for two fabulous fish cakes.

FISH AND CHIPS

POINTS	
per recipe: 28	per serving: 7

Serves: 4
Preparation time: 15 minutes
Cooking time: 50 minutes
Freezing: not recommended
Calories per serving: 400

Instead of frying – which adds fat and points – try this oven-baked version of one of Britain's best-loved dishes.

2 tablespoons olive oil
700 g (1 lb 9 oz) unpeeled potatoes, scrubbed and cut into wedges
4 × 175 g (6 oz) cod or haddock fillets
2 tablespoons plain white flour
1 medium egg
50 g (1³/₄ oz) dried breadcrumbs
salt and freshly ground black pepper
malt vinegar or lemon wedges, to serve

1 Preheat the oven to Gas Mark 6/ 200°C/400°F. Grease a roasting pan and a baking sheet with 1 teaspoon of the oil. Heat the roasting pan in the oven for 5 minutes.

2 Put the potato wedges in the roasting pan and sprinkle them with the remaining oil. Toss them together and then season with salt and pepper. Bake for about 30 minutes, until barely tender.

3 Meanwhile, rinse the fish fillets and pat them dry with kitchen paper. Sprinkle the flour on a plate, and season it with salt and pepper. Coat the fish fillets in the seasoned flour.

4 Beat the egg in a shallow bowl with 2 tablespoons of cold water. Sprinkle the breadcrumbs on a separate plate. Dip the floured fish fillets in the egg and then coat them in the breadcrumbs. Place the fillets on the prepared baking sheet.

5 Reduce the oven temperature to Gas Mark 5/190°C/375°F and continue to bake the potatoes, with the fish positioned on the shelf below them, for a further 15–20 minutes. Check that the fish is cooked by testing it with a fork – the flesh should be opaque and flake easily.

6 Serve the fish with the oven-baked wedges, seasoned with vinegar or lemon, salt and pepper.

VARIATION Try using coley or haddock instead of cod. They are more economical and will reduce the points to 6½ per serving.

MUSSELS IN WHITE WINE

POINTS	
per recipe: 8	per serving: 2

Serves: 4
Preparation time: 15 minutes
Cooking time: 15 minutes
Freezing: not recommended
Calories per serving: 120

Mussels are very low in points – making them a marvellous choice for a Weight Watchers meal. Farmed mussels are available all year round now – so why not make use of them more often? Serve the mussels with some slices of crusty French bread to mop up the delicious juices, remembering to add the extra points.

900 g (2 lb) mussels
1 tablespoon olive oil
1 small onion, chopped finely
2 garlic cloves, chopped finely
150 ml (¹/₄ pint) dry white wine
1¹/₄ tomatoes, skinned and chopped
150 ml (¹/₄ pint) vegetable or fish stock
freshly ground black pepper
2 tablespoons chopped fresh parsley or chives, to garnish

1 Scrub the mussels with a small stiff brush and scrape away their beards with a sharp knife. Throw away any damaged mussels or ones which remain open when tapped.

2 Heat the olive oil in a very large saucepan. Add the onion and garlic and sauté until softened – about 3 minutes. Add the wine and tomatoes, and heat until bubbling. Add the fish or vegetable stock. Allow to boil for a few minutes to reduce and concentrate the liquid.

3 Tip the mussels into the saucepan. Cover and cook for 3–4 minutes, until the shells have opened. Discard any mussels that remain shut.

4 Serve the mussels with the wine liquid, seasoned with black pepper and garnished with chopped fresh parsley or chives.

VARIATION For Thai-style mussels, add 1–2 teaspoons of Thai red or green curry paste with the stock in step 2, and use chopped fresh coriander instead of parsley or chives. The points will remain the same.

**Fish and Chips:
A terrific low
point version of
this traditional
supper.**

chicken & turkey

For healthy, low-fat meals, you can't beat chicken and turkey. They're so versatile too – forming the mainstay of so many tasty meals. You'll find lots of your favourite recipes here. Most of us love chicken – though sometimes we run short of inspiration. No fear – you'll find the ideal recipe here!

CHICKEN CASSEROLE

POINTS

per recipe: 12   per serving: 3

Serves: 4
Preparation time: 15 minutes
Cooking time: 1 hour 20 minutes
Freezing: recommended
Calories per serving: 240

What could be more welcoming than a delicious chicken casserole? Bake four medium jacket potatoes (225 g/8 oz each) in the oven while the casserole cooks. Add 2½ extra points per serving.

---

1 tablespoon vegetable oil

2 large onions, sliced

3 celery sticks, sliced

2 carrots, chopped

1 large leek, chopped

450 g (1 lb) skinless, boneless chicken breasts, cut into large chunks

150 ml (¼ pint) dry white wine

300 ml (½ pint) chicken stock

2 teaspoons dried mixed herbs

1 tablespoon cornflour

salt and freshly ground black pepper

---

1 Preheat the oven to Gas Mark 4/ 180°C/350°F.

2 Heat the vegetable oil in a large flameproof casserole, and sauté the onions, celery, carrots and leek for about 5 minutes, until softened.

3 Add the chicken to the casserole and cook until sealed on all sides. Add the wine and allow it to bubble up for a few moments. Pour in the chicken stock and add the dried mixed herbs. Season with a little salt and black pepper.

4 Place the lid on the casserole dish and transfer it to the middle shelf of the oven. Cook for 45 minutes.

5 Blend the cornflour with about 3 tablespoons of cold water to make a smooth paste. Add it to the casserole, stirring it in to mix well. Return the casserole to the oven to cook for a further 5 minutes.

6 Check the seasoning, adding more salt and pepper if needed and then serve on warmed plates.

VARIATION Omit the white wine if you prefer and use a total of 450 ml (16 fl oz) of chicken stock instead. This will reduce the points per serving to 2½.

**Chicken Casserole:
Warm yourself up
with this well-
loved dish.**

Chicken Fajitas with Salsa: Each delicious fajita is only 4½ points.

CHICKEN FAJITAS WITH SALSA

POINTS

per recipe: 18   per serving: 4½

Serves: 4
Preparation time: 15 minutes
Freezing: not recommended
Calories per serving: 270

Serve these with 75 g (2¾ oz) plain boiled rice if you are feeling very hungry but remember to add 1½ points per serving.

2 large tomatoes, chopped
¼ cucumber, chopped finely
1 small red onion, chopped finely
2 tablespoons chopped fresh coriander or mint
2 teaspoons lime or lemon juice
4 medium soft flour tortillas
175 g (6 oz) skinless, cooked chicken breast, torn into strips
4 tablespoons half-fat crème fraîche
25 g (1 oz) extra-mature Cheddar cheese, grated
salt and freshly ground black pepper

1 Preheat the oven to Gas Mark 2/ 150°C/300°F, if using in step 2. To make the salsa, mix together the tomatoes, cucumber, red onion and coriander or mint. Add the lime or lemon juice and season with salt and pepper.

2 Warm the tortillas in the oven or under a medium grill for 3–4 minutes.

3 Lay out the warm tortillas and spoon on some salsa. Divide the cooked chicken between them. Top with the crème fraîche and sprinkle with grated cheese, dividing the total amounts between the 4 tortillas. Roll up and serve with the remaining salsa.

CORONATION CHICKEN

POINTS

per recipe: 9½   per serving: 5

Serves: 2
Preparation time: 20 minutes
Freezing: not recommended
Calories per serving: 310

This version tastes superb. Serve with a side dish of halved cherry tomatoes and chopped spring onions, with fat-free dressing for no extra points.

100 g (3½ oz) 0% fat Greek plain yogurt or plain low-fat yogurt
1 teaspoon mild curry powder
2 teaspoons chopped fresh coriander or mint (optional)
1 medium banana, sliced
40 g (1½ oz) ready-to-eat dried apricots, chopped
15 g (½ oz) raisins or sultanas
225 g (8 oz) skinless, boneless roast chicken, sliced
salt and freshly ground black pepper
crisp lettuce leaves and cucumber slices, to serve
coriander and mint leaves, to garnish (optional)

1 In a large bowl, mix together the yogurt, curry powder and coriander or mint, if using.

2 Add the banana, apricots, raisins or sultanas. Mix in the chicken, stirring gently to coat in the curry sauce. Season to taste with salt and black pepper.

3 Arrange some lettuce leaves and cucumber slices on two serving plates and share out the chicken mixture between them. Garnish with a few coriander or mint leaves, if using. Serve at once.

1 Heat the vegetable oil in a large saucepan and sauté the onion and apple for 3–4 minutes. Add the garlic, carrot, parsnip and curry paste and cook, stirring, for 1 more minute.

2 Add the chicken to the saucepan and cook for 2–3 minutes, stirring often, until sealed.

3 Add the chicken stock, sultanas and chopped coriander or mint to the saucepan, stirring well. Bring up to simmering point and then partially cover and reduce the heat. Cook over a low heat for about 40 minutes.

4 About 15 minutes before the end of cooking time, cook the rice in plenty of lightly salted boiling water for about 12 minutes, until tender. Drain thoroughly and rinse with boiling water.

5 Slice the banana and stir it into the curry. Check the seasoning, adding salt and pepper, according to taste.

6 Serve the curry with the hot, cooked rice. Top each portion with one tablespoon of yogurt and garnish with fresh coriander or mint.

VARIATION Try using a Balti curry paste for a change. Points per serving will remain the same.

Instead of serving the yogurt plain, add about 2 tablespoons of finely chopped cucumber to make a refreshing raita.

Chicken Curry: A British favourite with rice for only 5½ points per serving.

CHICKEN CURRY

POINTS

per recipe: 22½	per serving: 5½

Serves: 4
Preparation time: 10 minutes
Cooking time: 55 minutes
Freezing: recommended
Calories per serving: 400

This fruity chicken curry is absolutely delicious. Choose mild, medium or hot curry paste – depending on how hot and spicy you want it to be.

2 teaspoons vegetable oil

1 large onion, chopped

1 medium apple, chopped

2 garlic cloves, crushed

1 large carrot, sliced

1 medium parsnip, chopped

2 tablespoons curry paste (mild, medium or hot, according to taste)

450 g (1 lb) skinless, boneless chicken breasts, cut into chunks

450 ml (16 fl oz) chicken stock

25g (1 oz) sultanas

1 tablespoon chopped fresh coriander or mint

150 g (5½ oz) basmati or long-grain rice

1 medium banana

salt and freshly ground black pepper

4 tablespoons plain low-fat yogurt, to serve

fresh coriander or mint sprigs, to garnish

TURKEY STIR-FRY

POINTS

per recipe: **5½**   per serving: **5½**

Ⓥ *if following the variation*

Serves: 1

Preparation time: 15 minutes

Cooking time: 10 minutes

Freezing: not recommended

Calories per serving: 410

Quick, colourful and very nutritious, this simple turkey stir-fry tastes superb.

---

40 g (1½ oz) Chinese thread or medium egg noodles

2 teaspoons stir-fry oil or vegetable oil

100 g (3½ oz) stir-fry turkey strips

3 spring onions, trimmed and sliced

½ red or yellow pepper, de-seeded and sliced finely

1 small carrot, cut into thin strips

2 celery sticks, sliced thinly

1 small garlic clove, crushed

25 g (1 oz) mushrooms, sliced

a generous pinch of Chinese five-spice powder

1 teaspoon chopped fresh coriander or chives

1 teaspoon light soy sauce

1 teaspoon sweet chilli sauce

salt and freshly ground black pepper

fresh coriander or chives, chopped, to garnish

1 Put the noodles in a bowl and cover with boiling water. Allow them to soak for 6 minutes, or follow the pack instructions.

2 Meanwhile, heat the oil in a wok or very large frying pan. Add the turkey and stir-fry briskly for 4–5 minutes.

3 Add the spring onions, pepper, carrot, celery and garlic. Stir-fry over a high heat for another 3–4 minutes, until the turkey is cooked. The vegetables should remain crisp and crunchy.

4 Drain the noodles thoroughly. Add them to the wok along with the mushrooms, five-spice powder, coriander or chives, soy sauce and chilli sauce. Stir-fry for 1–2 more minutes to heat thoroughly.

5 Season to taste with salt and black pepper and then serve in a warmed bowl, garnished with fresh coriander or chives.

TOP TIP If you prefer, omit the noodles and serve the stir-fry with 50 g (1¾ oz) of cooked long-grain rice. The points will be 4½.

VARIATION For a vegetarian version, leave out the turkey and add 100 g (3½ oz) of baby corn and 100 g (3½ oz) of mangetout or sugar snap peas to the wok with the spring onions. Points would be reduced to 2½ per serving.

Turkey Stir-fry: A delicious Oriental favourite.

**Chicken Kiev:
Served here with
low-fat chips for
a filling 7 point
meal.**

CHICKEN KIEV

POINTS

per recipe: 18½   per serving: 4½

Serves: 4
Preparation time: 20 minutes
Cooking time: 35–40 minutes
Calories per serving: 280
Freezing: recommended

Serve with 100 g (3½ oz) low-fat chips and zero-point vegetables such as fine green beans, cauliflower or carrots – or all three! Add 2½ points per serving.

low-fat cooking spray
4 medium, skinless, uncooked chicken breasts, each weighing about 150 g (5½ oz)
125 g tub low-fat soft cheese with garlic and herbs
2 tablespoons plain white flour
1 medium egg, beaten with 2 tablespoons cold water
50 g (1¾ oz) fresh white breadcrumbs
salt and freshly ground black pepper

1 Preheat the oven to Gas Mark 5/ 190°C/375°F. Mist a baking dish or baking sheet with low-fat cooking spray.
2 Put the chicken breasts, well spaced apart, between sheets of clingfilm or greaseproof paper. Use a meat mallet or rolling pin to beat them out until flattened, but avoid bashing them until they break up. Remove the clingfilm or paper.
3 Divide the soft cheese into four equal portions. Place the cheese portions on the chicken breasts, towards the wider end of the chicken. Season with salt and pepper. Roll up the breasts, folding in the sides to encase the cheese. Use cocktail sticks to secure them.
4 Roll the chicken parcels in the flour and then dip them into the beaten egg mixture. Finally, roll them in the breadcrumbs and place in the dish or on the baking sheet.
5 Bake for 35–40 minutes, until golden brown and thoroughly cooked. To check, pierce the chicken with a skewer or sharp knife – the juices should run clear. Remove the cocktail sticks before serving.

VARIATION For an extra garlic hit, spread ½ teaspoon of garlic purée over each chicken breast before adding the cheese. The points will remain the same.

SWEET & SOUR CHICKEN

POINTS

per recipe: 19   per serving: 5

Ⓥ if following variation
Serves: 4
Preparation and cooking time: 30 minutes
Calories per serving: 375
Freezing: not recommended

Stir-fry strips of chicken taste fabulous in this quick and easy dish.

150 g (5½ oz) long-grain rice
210 g can pineapple chunks in natural juice
2 teaspoons chilli sauce
2 tablespoons light soy sauce
2 tablespoons seasoned rice vinegar dressing or cider vinegar
1 tablespoon light muscovado sugar
1 tablespoon cornflour
2 teaspoons Chinese five-spice powder
1 tablespoon stir-fry oil or vegetable oil
350 g (12 oz) skinless, boneless chicken breasts, cut into chunks
1 large red onion, sliced
1 yellow pepper, de-seeded and cut into chunks
100 g (3½ oz) mangetout or sugar snap peas, halved
3 celery sticks, sliced
4 medium tomatoes, sliced into wedges
salt and freshly ground black pepper

TO GARNISH
fresh red chilli or red pepper, de-seeded and sliced thinly
chopped fresh coriander or parsley

1 Cook the rice in plenty of lightly salted boiling water for about 12 minutes, or until tender.
2 Meanwhile, drain the juice from the pineapples into a small bowl or jug. Add the chilli sauce, soy sauce, seasoned rice vinegar dressing or cider vinegar, sugar, cornflour and five-spice powder. Set to one side.
3 Heat the oil in a wok or very large frying pan. Add the chicken, a handful at a time, and stir-fry over a high heat for 3–4 minutes.
4 Add the onion, pepper, mangetout or sugar snap peas and celery to the wok. Stir-fry for another 3–4 minutes. Then add the tomatoes and pineapple.
5 Give the pineapple juice mixture a good stir and then add it to the wok, stirring until hot and thickened. Season to taste with salt and pepper, adding a little more soy sauce and chilli sauce, if you like.
6 Serve with the rice, garnished with the thinly sliced chilli or pepper and fresh coriander or parsley.

VARIATION For a vegetarian version, omit the chicken and use 350 g (12 oz) of Quorn pieces instead. The points will be 4½ per serving.

It's wonderful that when you're following **pure points**™, you can still tuck in to your favourite food. There's nothing more disheartening than seeing the rest of the family enjoy the food they love, while you try to look enthusiastic over a bowlful of salad leaves. So take heart – and delve into this chapter for recipes that will please your family and please you.

SAUSAGES IN MUSHROOM AND ONION GRAVY WITH PARSLEY MASH

POINTS

per recipe: 12   per serving: 6

V *if following the variation*
Serves: 2
Preparation and cooking time: 35 minutes
Freezing: not recommended
Calories per serving: 295

You won't feel like you're trying to lose weight when you tuck into a plateful of sausages and mash – it's the ultimate comfort food.

350 g (12 oz) potatoes, peeled and quartered

175 g (6 oz) reduced-fat pork and beef sausages

4 rounded teaspoons instant gravy granules

1 onion, chopped

1 tablespoon medium sherry

50 g (1³/₄ oz) button mushrooms

1 teaspoon mushroom ketchup or Worcestershire sauce

1 teaspoon dried mixed Italian herbs

3 tablespoons skimmed milk

1 tablespoon chopped fresh parsley

salt and freshly ground black pepper

1 Cook the potatoes in a large saucepan of lightly salted simmering water for about 20 minutes, until they are tender.

2 Meanwhile, cook the sausages over a medium heat in a large non-stick frying pan without adding any more fat to the pan. Turn them often until they are well browned.

3 To make the gravy, mix the gravy granules into 300 ml (½ pint) of boiling water.

4 Add the onion to the frying pan. Cook for 2–3 minutes, and then add the gravy, sherry, mushrooms, mushroom ketchup or Worcestershire sauce and dried herbs. Heat and simmer gently for 5 minutes. Season to taste with salt and pepper.

5 Drain the potatoes and mash well. Add the milk and parsley. Season and beat vigorously with a wooden spoon to make the potatoes light and fluffy.

6 Reheat the mash over a low heat, stirring constantly to prevent it from sticking. Serve with the sausages and gravy.

VARIATIONS For a delicious change, make the mash with 150 g (5½ oz) potato and 150 g (5½ oz) swede or butternut squash – just cook the two vegetables together. Points per serving will be reduced to 5.

For a vegetarian version, use vegetarian sausages and vegetarian gravy granules in this recipe. The points per serving will be 5½.

Sausages in Mushroom and Onion Gravy with Parsley Mash: What could be better for only 6 points?

Toad-in-the-Hole:
It's well worth saving
up points for this
incredibly satisfying
and delicious supper.

TOAD-IN-THE-HOLE

POINTS

per recipe: 22   per serving: 5½

Serves: 4
Preparation time: 20 minutes
Cooking time: 40 minutes
Freezing: not recommended
Calories per serving: 355

Toad-in-the-hole is a great favourite with all the family. Serve this dish with fresh green zero-point vegetables, such as broccoli or green beans.

125 g (4½ oz) plain white flour
½ teaspoon salt
1 large egg
300 ml (½ pint) skimmed milk
2 tablespoons vegetable oil
350 g (12 oz) 95% fat-free thin sausages or chipolatas
1 teaspoon butter
1 onion, sliced thinly
4 rounded teaspoons instant gravy granules
salt and freshly ground black pepper

1 To make the batter, put the flour, salt, egg and milk in a large mixing bowl with 2 tablespoons (30 ml) of cold water. Beat together, using a wire whisk or a hand-held electric beater. Allow to stand for 10–15 minutes.
2 Preheat the oven to Gas Mark 7/ 220°C/425°F.
3 Put the oil and the sausages in a medium-sized non-stick roasting pan (approximately 23 cm 2 18 cm/ 9-inch 27-inch) and heat in the oven for about 3–4 minutes, until very hot.
4 Pour the batter around the sausages and return the roasting pan to the oven as quickly as possible. Bake for 25–30 minutes or until risen and golden brown.

5 Meanwhile, make the onion gravy. Melt the butter in a saucepan and add the onion, cooking over a low heat until golden brown.
6 Add 300 ml (½ pint) of water to the pan. Heat until simmering and then stir in the gravy granules. Cook until thickened. Season to taste. Serve the toad-in-the-hole with the gravy.

TOP TIP Avoid opening the oven door until at least 20 minutes have elapsed, or else the batter could deflate.

VARIATION Make individual servings by cooking the sausages and batter in large Yorkshire pudding tins.

BURGERS IN BUNS

POINTS

per recipe: 25½   per serving: 6½

Ⓥ if following the variation
Serves: 4
Preparation and cooking time: 20 minutes
Freezing: recommended prior to cooking
Calories per serving: 350

Home-made burgers are simple to make and delicious to eat – and you can use your favourite type of mince (see variations for points).

450 g (1 lb) very lean minced beef
1 small onion, chopped very finely
2 tablespoons chopped fresh parsley or coriander
2 teaspoons dried mixed herbs
a few drops of chilli sauce, mushroom ketchup or Worcestershire sauce
1 small egg, beaten
salt and freshly ground black pepper

TO SERVE

4 standard burger buns
shredded lettuce, sliced gherkins and tomatoes

1 In a large bowl, combine all the burger ingredients together until thoroughly mixed.
2 Shape the mixture into four burgers. Wrap in clingfilm and refrigerate until required.
3 Preheat the grill. Then grill the burgers for about 10 minutes, turning once, until browned and cooked through.

4 Lightly toast the burger buns on the cut sides only and then top with plenty of shredded lettuce. Add the burgers and garnish with sliced gherkins and tomatoes.

VARIATIONS Make a vegetarian burger by using Quorn mince instead of meat. Points per serving will be 4.

Substitute the beef with turkey, pork or lamb. The points, respectively will be 5, 6 and 7 per serving.

Spice up the burgers by adding half a teaspoon of de-seeded, finely chopped fresh red or green chilli – or add a generous pinch of chilli powder instead.

Steak and Kidney Pie: A true British favourite.

STEAK AND KIDNEY PIE

POINTS

per recipe: 45   per serving: 7½

Serves: 6
Preparation time: 20 minutes
Cooking time: 2½ hours
Freezing: recommended
Calories per serving: 390

Mushrooms and sherry give a rich flavour to this classic British dish. If you don't eat any of the puff pastry topping, you'll be saving yourself 3½ points per serving.

2 teaspoons vegetable oil

700 g (1 lb 9 oz) lean stewing steak, cubed

2 × 25 g (1 oz) lamb's kidneys, trimmed and chopped

1 large onion, chopped

1 beef stock cube, dissolved in 450 ml (16 fl oz) hot water

2 tablespoons medium sherry

225 g (8 oz) mushrooms, sliced

1 tablespoon chopped fresh parsley

2 tablespoons cornflour, blended with 3-4 tablespoons cold water

225 g (8 oz) frozen puff pastry sheet, defrosted

1 tablespoon skimmed milk

salt and freshly ground black pepper

1 Heat the oil in a large saucepan and over a high heat add the cubes of stewing steak a handful at a time, so that they seal and brown. Add the kidneys, stir well and then reduce the heat a little. Add the onion and cook for another 3–4 minutes, until softened.

2 Add the stock, sherry, mushrooms and parsley to the saucepan. Bring up to the boil and then reduce the heat. Cover and simmer for 1½ hours, until the meat is very tender. Check the level of liquid from time to time, topping up with a little extra water if necessary.

3 Preheat the oven to Gas Mark 7/ 220°C/425°F

4 Season the cooked meat with salt and pepper. Add the blended cornflour and stir until thickened. Cook for 1 minute and then tip the mixture into an oblong baking dish.

5 Lay the puff pastry sheet on top of the baking dish, trimming the edges with a sharp knife. Use the trimmings to make leaves for decoration. Position them on top, and brush the entire surface with milk. Bake for 25–30 minutes, until puffed up and golden brown.

LIVER AND BACON

POINTS

per recipe: 27½   per serving: 7

Serves: 4
Preparation time: 10 minutes
Cooking time: 20 minutes
Freezing: not recommended
Calories per serving: 285

Liver and bacon always makes such a welcome, tasty meal – and for economy, it fits the bill perfectly. Serve this warming dish with mashed potatoes and lots of fresh vegetables, remembering to add the extra points. 1 scoop (60 g) of mash is 1 point.

500 g (1 lb 2 oz) lamb's liver, trimmed and sliced thinly

2 tablespoons plain white flour

1 teaspoon dried mixed herbs

1 tablespoon vegetable oil

2 rashers of lean back bacon, snipped into pieces

2 onions, sliced thinly into rings

300 ml (½ pint) lamb or chicken stock

salt and freshly ground black pepper

1 Rinse the liver and pat dry with kitchen paper.

2 Sprinkle the flour on a plate and season well with salt, black pepper and the dried mixed herbs. Coat the liver in this seasoned flour.

3 Heat the vegetable oil in a large frying pan and add the bacon and onions. Sauté for about 5–8 minutes, until the onions are softened and browned and the bacon is crispy.

4 Add the liver to the frying pan and cook for 1–2 minutes on each side. Pour in the stock and bring to the boil, stirring constantly. Reduce the heat and simmer gently for about 3–4 minutes and serve. Avoid overcooking the liver, or else it will become tough.

VARIATION Try using dried mixed Italian herbs instead of ordinary ones, or add a teaspoon of dried, crushed rosemary to the flour for a delicious flavour.

CHILLI CON CARNE

POINTS

per recipe: **26**   **per serving: 6½**

Ⓥ if following the variation

Serves: 4
Preparation time: 10 minutes
Cooking time: 40 minutes
Freezing: recommended
Calories per serving: 475

Make this very tasty chilli with more vegetables and a little less meat than usual. You'll soon have a delicious meal, with fewer points.

350 g (12 oz) very lean minced beef
1 large onion, chopped
2 garlic cloves, crushed
1 courgette, chopped finely
1 large carrot, chopped finely
1 red or green pepper, de-seeded and chopped
2–3 teaspoons medium chilli powder
400 g can chopped tomatoes
2 tablespoons tomato purée
400 g can red kidney beans, rinsed and drained
300 ml (½ pint) beef or vegetable stock
200 g (7 oz) long-grain rice
salt and freshly ground black pepper

1 Heat a large non-stick saucepan and add the mince, a handful at a time, so that it seals and browns.

2 Add the onion, garlic, courgette, carrot, pepper, chilli powder, tomatoes, tomato purée, red kidney beans and stock. Stir well and bring to the boil. Cover and reduce the heat. Simmer for about 30 minutes, stirring from time to time.

3 Fifteen minutes before you're ready to serve, put the rice on to cook. Boil the rice in plenty of lightly salted boiling water until tender, about 12 minutes. Drain well and rinse with boiling water.

4 Check the seasoning of the chilli, adding salt and pepper according to taste. Divide the cooked rice between four warm serving plates and pile the cooked chilli on top. Serve at once.

TOP TIP Remember to cook spicy food according to your taste. Add more chilli powder or use a hotter variety if you like things spicy. Use less or a milder type if you prefer.

VARIATIONS For a change, omit the rice and fill eight soft flour tortillas with the chilli instead. Bake at Gas Mark 5/190°C/375°F for 20 minutes, or until the tortillas are light brown and crispy. Points per serving will be 8. Serve with shredded lettuce, onion, cucumber and tomato.

For a vegetarian version, use 350 g (12 oz) Quorn mince instead of minced beef, and use vegetable stock. The points per serving will be 4½.

SPAGHETTI CARBONARA

POINTS

per recipe: **13½**   **per serving: 7**

Serves: 2
Preparation time: 10 minutes
Cooking time: 15 minutes
Freezing: not recommended
Calories per serving: 400

You can use spaghetti, fettuccine or tagliatelle to make this Carbonara.

110 g (4 oz) spaghetti, fettuccine or tagliatelle
1 teaspoon olive oil
½ small onion, chopped finely
1 small garlic clove, peeled and left whole
100 g (3½ oz) low-fat soft cheese
1 egg
5 tablespoons skimmed milk
25 g (1 oz) Parma ham or lean boiled ham, cut into strips
15 g (½ oz) finely grated Parmesan cheese
2 teaspoons chopped fresh oregano or parsley
salt and freshly ground black pepper
fresh oregano or parsley sprigs, to garnish

1 Cook the spaghetti, fettuccine or tagliatelle in plenty of lightly salted boiling water for 12 minutes, or according to pack instructions.

2 While the pasta is cooking, heat the oil in a frying pan and sauté the onion and garlic clove for about 5 minutes, until softened. Discard the garlic clove.

3 Put the soft cheese in a mixing bowl and beat with a wooden spoon to soften it. Add the egg and onion, stirring until combined. Add the milk, ham, Parmesan cheese and the oregano or parsley. Season with salt and pepper.

4 Drain the pasta, reserving a couple of tablespoons of the cooking liquid and then return it to the saucepan with the reserved liquid. Add the egg mixture and heat gently for 2–3 minutes, stirring, until the mixture has cooked and thickened.

5 Serve garnished with sprigs of oregano or parsley.

1 Heat a large, non-stick frying pan and then add the pork mince a handful at a time to seal and brown it. Add the onion and garlic, cook for a minute or two. Add the dried herbs and stock.

2 Simmer for 10 minutes and then add the blended cornflour. Cook, stirring until thickened. Season to taste. Cool for about 10 minutes.

3 Put the soft cheese in a mixing bowl, beat with a wooden spoon to soften it. Stir in the yogurt, half the Parmesan cheese and a little salt and pepper.

4 Preheat the oven to Gas Mark 4/ 180°C/350°F.

5 Mist a shallow, ovenproof dish with low-fat cooking spray. Pour half the tomato pasta sauce in the dish. Spoon the mince mixture into the cannelloni tubes. Arrange the tubes in the baking dish and pour over the remaining pasta sauce. Top with the soft cheese mixture and sprinkle with the remaining Parmesan cheese.

6 Bake for 40–45 minutes, until golden brown and bubbling.

VARIATIONS Try using turkey mince instead of pork – points will be 5½ per serving.

If you're vegetarian, use Quorn mince – points will be 5 per serving.

Cannelloni: A classic pasta dish for only 5½ points.

CANNELLONI

POINTS

per recipe: 22   per serving: 5½

Ⓥ *if following variation*
Serves: 4
Preparation time: 30 minutes
Cooking time: 45 minutes
Freezing: recommended
Calories per serving: 365

Serve the cannelloni with a large, mixed green salad with fat-free dressing for a zero-point accompaniment.

225 g (8 oz) lean pork mince

1 small onion, chopped finely

1 garlic clove, crushed

1 teaspoon mixed dried Italian herbs

1 pork or chicken stock cube, dissolved in 150 ml (¼ pint) hot water

1 tablespoon cornflour, blended with 2–3 tablespoons cold water

200 g tub low-fat soft cheese (with garlic and herbs, preferably)

150 g (5½ oz) plain low-fat yogurt

25 g (1 oz) finely grated Parmesan cheese

low-fat cooking spray

320 g jar spicy tomato pasta sauce

16 × 150 g (5½ oz) cannelloni tubes (choose ones that need no pre-cooking)

salt and freshly ground black pepper

CLASSIC BEEF STEW WITH DUMPLINGS

POINTS

per recipe: 27½   per serving: 7

Serves: 4
Preparation time: 20 minutes
Cooking time: 2 hours 10 minutes
Freezing: recommended
Calories per serving: 410

To save points, you can make the casserole without the dumplings. Points would be reduced to 4½. Serve with lightly cooked cabbage and some broccoli for no extra points.

1 tablespoon vegetable oil
500 g (1 lb 2 oz) lean braising steak, cut into chunks
8 shallots or small onions, halved
3 celery sticks, chopped
2 medium carrots, sliced
1 turnip, chopped
2 medium parsnips, cut into chunks
450 ml (16 fl oz) beef stock
1 bay leaf
1 teaspoon dried mixed herbs
salt and freshly ground black pepper

FOR THE DUMPLINGS

100 g (3½ oz) self-raising flour
a pinch of salt
1 teaspoon dried mixed herbs
2 tablespoons polyunsaturated margarine
1 tablespoon horseradish sauce

1 Preheat the oven to Gas Mark 3/ 170°C/325°F.

2 Heat the oil in a large, flameproof casserole dish and add the braising steak, a handful at a time, cooking over a high heat until sealed and browned.

3 Add the shallots or onions, celery, carrots, turnip and parsnips, and cook for about 5 minutes. Add the stock, bay leaf and herbs. Season with salt and pepper. Transfer to the oven and cook for 1½ hours.

4 Next, make the dumplings. Sift the flour and salt into a bowl and mix in the dried herbs. Rub in the margarine until the mixture resembles fine breadcrumbs. Stir in the horseradish sauce and just enough cold water to make a soft, but not sticky dough. Form into eight small dumplings and add to the casserole. Cover and cook for a further 30 minutes, or until the meat is tender.

5 Serve the casserole, removing the bay leaf. Allow two dumplings per portion.

Classic Beef Stew with Dumplings: The ultimate in comfort food.

SHEPHERD'S PIE

POINTS

per recipe: 27½   per serving: 7

V *if following the variation*

Serves 4
Preparation time: 20 minutes
Cooking time: 1 hour
Freezing: recommended
Calories per serving: 390

Serve with plenty of point-free vegetables: broccoli, cauliflower or cabbage would be ideal.

900 g (2 lb) potatoes, peeled and quartered
350 g (12 oz) lean, minced lamb
1 large onion, chopped finely
1 large leek, chopped finely
1 carrot, chopped
225 g (8 oz) swede or turnip, chopped
450 ml (16 fl oz) lamb or vegetable stock
2 tablespoons cornflour, blended with 3 or 4 tablespoons cold water
6 tablespoons skimmed milk
salt and freshly ground black pepper

1 Cook the potatoes in lightly salted boiling water for about 20 minutes, until tender.
2 Meanwhile, heat a large, non-stick saucepan and add the lamb mince, a handful at a time, cooking over a high heat to seal and brown it.
3 Add the onion to the mince with the leek, carrot and swede or turnip and cook for about 3 minutes, stirring often. Pour in the stock, bring to the boil. Cover and simmer for about 20 minutes.
4 Preheat the oven to Gas Mark 5/ 190°C/375°F.
5 Stir the blended cornflour into the minced lamb mixture. Cook until thickened for about 2 minutes. Remove from the heat.
6 Drain the potatoes and mash them. Add the milk and seasoning and beat vigorously with a wooden spoon until the potatoes are light and fluffy. Alternatively, use a hand-held electric beater to whisk the potatoes for a few moments.
7 Transfer the meat mixture to a 1.2 litre (2-pint) ovenproof dish and top with the mashed potato. Bake for 25–30 minutes until thoroughly heated and browned.

VARIATIONS Before baking in the oven, sprinkle the surface of the mash with finely sliced leek and 25 g (1 oz) of grated mature Cheddar. Points per serving will be 7½.

For a vegetarian version, use Quorn mince instead of lamb and be sure to use vegetable stock. The points per serving will be reduced to 4½.

SPARE RIBS

POINTS

per recipe: 32   per serving: 8

Serves: 4
Preparation time: 10 minutes
Cooking time: 1 hour
Freezing: not recommended
Calories per serving: 225

These spare ribs are well worth saving the points for. Serve with a zero-point salad for a delicious dinner.

750 g (1 lb 10 oz) lean pork spare ribs
1 tablespoon clear honey
2 tablespoons tomato purée
2 tablespoons lemon juice
3 tablespoons soy sauce
3 tablespoons oyster sauce
1 teaspoon Chinese five-spice powder
salt and freshly ground black pepper

TO GARNISH
4 spring onions, sliced finely
4 tomatoes, cut into wedges.

1 Preheat the oven to Gas Mark 6/ 200°C/400°F.
2 Put the spare ribs in a large roasting pan. Mix together the honey, tomato purée, lemon juice, soy sauce, oyster sauce and Chinese five-spice powder. Season with salt and pepper and pour over the ribs, tossing them to coat in the mixture. Roast for 50 minutes–1 hour until tender.
3 Serve the spare ribs sprinkled with the sliced spring onions. Garnish with the tomatoes.

VARIATION If you like your spare ribs to be spicy-hot, add a teaspoon of hot chilli sauce to the honey mixture in step two.

Shepherd's Pie:
Enjoy this family
favourite and
still lose weight
– the family will
never guess it's
lower in points.

vegetarian classics

More and more people are eating vegetarian meals as a healthy addition to a sensible, well-balanced diet – regardless of whether they eat vegetarian food the rest of the week. All the recipes in this chapter are tasty and nutritious, and they are quick and easy to put together – an important fact when you consider how busy we all are.

VEGETABLE LASAGNE

POINTS

per recipe: 20½   per serving: 5

V *if using vegetarian cheese*
Serves: 4
Preparation time: 20 minutes
Cooking time: 55 minutes
Calories per serving: 355
Freezing: recommended

This colourful lasagne makes a healthy and delicious vegetarian meal. Serve with a chopped tomato and onion salad for a colourful, point-free accompaniment.

1 tablespoon olive oil
1 medium onion, chopped
1 medium courgette, sliced
1 medium red pepper, de-seeded and chopped
1 medium yellow or green pepper, de-seeded and chopped
225 g (8 oz) mushrooms, sliced
320 g jar of tomato pasta sauce

1 teaspoon dried mixed Italian herbs
300 ml (½ pint) skimmed milk
25 g (1 oz) plain white flour
1 tablespoon polyunsaturated margarine
50 g (1¾ oz) extra-mature Cheddar cheese, grated
125 g (4½ oz) no pre-cook lasagne sheets (6 sheets)
salt and freshly ground black pepper

1 Preheat the oven to Gas Mark 5/190°C/375°F.
2 Heat the oil in a large frying pan or wok and sauté the onion until softened – about 3–4 minutes. Add the courgette, peppers and mushrooms, and stir-fry for another 2 minutes or so. Tip in the pasta sauce and dried herbs and season with salt and pepper. Remove from the heat.
3 Make the cheese sauce by the all-in-one method. To do this, put the milk, flour and margarine in a medium saucepan. Bring to the boil, stirring constantly with a wire whisk, until the sauce blends and thickens.

Add the cheese and cook gently for about 30 seconds, stirring until melted. Season to taste with salt and pepper.
4 Spoon half the vegetable mixture into an oblong ovenproof dish and lay half the lasagne sheets on top. Spread 3–4 tablespoons of the cheese sauce over the lasagne and then add the remaining vegetable mixture. Cover with the rest of the lasagne sheets and spread the rest of the cheese sauce on top.
5 Transfer to the oven and bake for 40–45 minutes, until golden brown.

VARIATIONS Vary the vegetables according to your own preferences, for instance if you're not keen on mushrooms, use a small aubergine instead.

To reduce the points to 4½ per serving, omit the Cheddar cheese from the sauce and sprinkle the surface of the lasagne with 2 tablespoons of finely grated Parmesan cheese, just before baking.

Vegetable Lasagne: Lasagne is definitely one of the all-time favourite dishes – and deservedly so!

Cheese, Onion and Tomato Quiche: Impress friends and family with this classic luncheon dish.

CHEESE, ONION AND TOMATO QUICHE

POINTS

per recipe: 19½   per serving: 5

(v) if using vegetarian cheese

Serves: 4

Preparation time: 20 minutes

Cooking time: 30 minutes

Freezing: recommended

Calories per serving: 350

Filo pastry gives a new slant to an old favourite, and helps to keep the points under control. Serve with a large mixed salad with fat-free dressing for no extra points.

FOR THE PASTRY

8 sheets fresh filo pastry

2 tablespoons delicately flavoured or light olive oil

FOR THE FILLING

2 teaspoons olive oil

2 large onions, sliced into rings

3 large tomatoes, sliced

2 medium eggs

150 ml (¼ pint) skimmed milk

1 tablespoon chopped fresh mixed herbs, or 1 teaspoon dried mixed herbs

40 g (1½ oz) mature Cheddar cheese, grated

salt and freshly ground black pepper

1 Preheat the oven to Gas Mark 2/ 150°C/300°F.

2 Unroll the sheets of filo pastry, keeping them covered with clingfilm or a damp cloth as you work to prevent them drying out. Brush each one with a little olive oil and layer them in a 20 cm (8-inch) flan tin. Stand the flan tin on a baking sheet.

3 For the filling, heat the oil in a frying pan and sauté the onions until softened, about 5 minutes. Tip them into the flan case and spread them over the base. Top with the sliced tomatoes.

4 Beat together the eggs, milk and herbs. Season with salt and pepper and pour into the flan case. Sprinkle with the cheese and bake for 20–25 minutes on the middle shelf until set. Cool slightly before serving.

VARIATION If you're not keen on tomatoes, use a couple of sliced medium courgettes or 175 g (6 oz) of lightly cooked asparagus instead. Points per serving will remain the same.

CAULIFLOWER CHEESE

POINTS

per recipe: 5½   per serving: 5½

(v) if using vegetarian cheese

Serves: 1

Preparation and cooking time: 20 minutes

Freezing: not recommended

Calories per serving: 270

This quick and easy favourite always goes down a treat.

½ small cauliflower, broken into florets

150 ml (¼ pint) skimmed milk

1 tablespoon plain white flour

1 teaspoon polyunsaturated margarine

25 g (1 oz) extra-mature Cheddar cheese, grated

1 teaspoon wholegrain mustard

salt and freshly ground black pepper

chopped fresh parsley, to garnish (optional)

1 Cook the cauliflower in a saucepan with a small amount of boiling, lightly salted water until just tender – about 10 minutes.

2 Meanwhile, make the cheese sauce by the all-in-one method. To do this, put the milk, flour and margarine in a small saucepan. Bring to the boil, stirring constantly with a wire whisk, until the sauce blends and thickens. Turn down the heat to low and cook gently, stirring all the time, for another 30 seconds or so.

3 Add the cheese and mustard to the sauce and cook gently for about 30 seconds, stirring, until the cheese has melted. Season to taste with salt and pepper.

4 Drain the cauliflower really well and tip out on to a warmed plate. Pour over the sauce and eat at once. Garnish with the fresh parsley, if using.

VARIATIONS Use cheese with a well-developed flavour for the best results. Try Cotswold cheese which is Double Gloucester with onion and chives for a different flavour. Points will remain the same.

Try using half cauliflower and half broccoli florets for a change.

VEGETABLE CURRY

POINTS

per recipe: 6   **per serving:** 3

Ⓥ Serves: 2

Preparation time: 20 minutes
Cooking time: 30 minutes
Freezing: not recommended
Calories per serving: 235

You'll be amazed at just how delicious
this healthy vegetable curry is – and
it's so low in points! If you serve
each portion of curry with half a
medium naan bread you will add 4
points. One chappati made without
fat will add 1½ Points, and a small
portion (75 g/2¾ oz) of cooked
long-grain rice will add 1½ points.

2 teaspoons olive oil

1 small onion, sliced

1 small garlic clove, crushed

½ aubergine, cut into chunks

*¼ medium butternut squash, peeled,
de-seeded and cut into chunks*

450 ml (16 fl oz) hot vegetable stock

1 red pepper, de-seeded and chopped

1 small courgette, sliced

½ small cauliflower, broken into florets

50 g (1¾ oz) baby corn, halved

*1½ tablespoons balti or medium
curry paste*

*1 tablespoon cornflour, blended with
2–3 tablespoons of water*

salt and freshly ground black pepper

FOR THE RAITA

150 ml (¼ pint) low-fat plain yogurt

*5 cm (2-inch) piece of cucumber,
chopped finely*

*1 tablespoon chopped fresh coriander
or mint*

1 Heat the olive oil in a large
saucepan and add the onion. Sauté
gently for about 3–4 minutes until
softened. Add the garlic and cook
for another minute.

2 Add the aubergine, butternut squash
and vegetable stock to the saucepan.
Bring to the boil and then reduce the
heat. Add all the remaining vegetables
and stir in the curry paste. Cook
for about 15 minutes, so that the
vegetables are tender yet retain
some 'bite'.

3 While the vegetables are cooking,
make the raita by mixing together
the yogurt, cucumber and coriander
or mint.

4 Stir the blended cornflour into the
curry. Cook for a couple of minutes
until thickened. Taste and season
with salt and pepper.

5 Serve the curry, accompanied by
the cucumber raita.

VARIATION Butternut squash tastes
delicious in this curry, but if you
can't find one use a quarter of a
large parsnip instead. The points
will remain the same.

Vegetable Curry:
A delicious low-
point curry with
rice for only 4½
points.

1 Preheat the grill to a medium heat.

2 In a small bowl, mix together the soft cheese and Caerphilly, mushroom ketchup or soy sauce and mustard. Season with a little black pepper.

3 Lightly toast the bread on both sides. Spread the cheese mixture on top, and then grill until golden and bubbling.

4 Serve at once with the tomatoes, garnished with salad leaves, if using.

VARIATIONS Use plain low-fat soft cheese if you prefer and, if you want to spice up your Welsh rarebit, add a few drops of chilli sauce instead of the mushroom ketchup or soy sauce.

For a more substantial meal, top with well-drained lightly cooked spinach and a poached egg. Points per serving will be 4.

Welsh Rarebit: The most famous cheese-on-toast dish.

WELSH RAREBIT

POINTS	
per recipe: 10	per serving: 2½

Ⓥ *if using vegetarian cheese*
Serves: 4
Preparation and cooking time: 20 minutes
Freezing: not recommended
Calories per serving: 140

It's hard to find a more classic combination than simple toast with cheese. This recipe is recognised all over the world as one of the great simple dishes. It's quick, easy to make and inexpensive, so it's a favourite with families. But because cheese can be high in points, you may be wary of it when trying to lose weight. However, there is no need to worry with this version, it's just as tasty as ever but much lower in points.

100 g (3½ oz) low-fat soft cheese with garlic and herbs

40 g (1½ oz) Caerphilly or mature Cheddar cheese, grated finely

a few drops of mushroom ketchup or soy sauce

½ teaspoon wholegrain mustard

4 × 25 g (1 oz) slices of white or wholemeal bread

freshly ground black pepper

4 tomatoes, sliced, to serve

salad leaves, to garnish (optional)

MACARONI CHEESE

POINTS

per recipe: 28½ | per serving: 7

Ⓥ *if using vegetarian cheese*

Serves: 4

Preparation time:10 minutes

Cooking time: 20 minutes

Freezing: recommended

Calories per serving: 415

Why not just have half a portion of this macaroni cheese for a light meal to reduce the points per serving to 4. Serve with a large green salad tossed in fat-free dressing for no extra points and you'll still feel full.

175 g (6 oz) macaroni or pasta tubes

25 g (1 oz) polyunsaturated margarine

40 g (1½ oz) plain white flour

450 ml (16 fl oz) skimmed milk

100 g (3½ oz) extra-mature Cheddar cheese, grated

1 heaped teaspoon wholegrain mustard

4 tomatoes, sliced

1 slice of bread from a large thick-sliced loaf, cut into cubes

salt and freshly ground black pepper

1 Cook the macaroni or pasta tubes in a large saucepan of lightly salted, boiling water for about 10–12 minutes until just tender, or follow the pack instructions.

2 Meanwhile, make an all-in-one sauce by putting the margarine, flour and milk into a medium saucepan. Heat, stirring all the time with a small wire whisk, until the sauce boils and thickens. Reduce the heat and cook gently for another minute. Remove from the heat and add most of the cheese, reserving a little for the topping. Let it melt in the heat of the sauce.

3 Preheat the grill to a medium-high heat and warm a 1.5 litre (2¾-pint) heatproof dish.

4 Add the mustard to the sauce and season with salt and pepper. Drain the macaroni thoroughly and add it to the warmed dish. Pour over the cheese sauce, stirring it into the macaroni.

5 Arrange the tomatoes over the top of the macaroni cheese. Scatter the bread cubes and reserved cheese over the surface. Grill for about 5 minutes until bubbling and golden brown.

VARIATION You don't have to use macaroni – just use your own favourite pasta, though a shape which holds sauce well works best.

Macaroni Cheese: So satisfyingly good!

ROASTED MEDITERRANEAN VEGETABLES

POINTS

per recipe: 9½	per serving: 2½

Ⓥ Serves: 4
Preparation time: 10 minutes
Cooking time: 45 minutes
Calories per serving: 265
Freezing: not recommended

These colourful vegetables taste fantastic; the roasting concentrates their flavours beautifully. They make a healthy meal – and they're very low in points.

2 tablespoons olive oil

175 g (6 oz) baby new potatoes, halved

3 red onions, each cut into 8 wedges

4 small parsnips, quartered lengthways

1 large butternut squash, peeled, de-seeded and cut into chunks

2 large courgettes, sliced

1 red and 1 yellow pepper, de-seeded and cut into chunks

½ teaspoon cumin seeds (optional)

fresh thyme and rosemary sprigs

16 cherry tomatoes

salt and freshly ground black pepper

basil leaves, to garnish

1 Preheat the oven to Gas Mark 6/ 200°C/400°F.
2 Pour the olive oil into a roasting pan and add the new potatoes, red onions, parsnips, butternut squash, courgettes and peppers. Season with salt and pepper, add the cumin seeds, if using, and then toss together so that all the vegetables are coated with the oil. Add the sprigs of thyme and rosemary.
3 Roast for 30 minutes. Add the tomatoes and roasted for another 10–15 minutes, or until the vegetables are tender.
4 Serve garnished with basil leaves.

TOP TIP These roasted vegetables taste fantastic served with some mango chutney and half-fat crème fraîche on the side. A tablespoon of each would add 1½ points per serving.

VARIATIONS If you can't find a butternut squash, use 2 aubergines instead.

Cumin seeds add a wonderful aroma and flavour, though you could add 2 teaspoons of dried oregano as an alternative.

CLASSIC OMELETTE

POINTS

per recipe: 13	per serving: 6½

Ⓥ if using vegetarian cheese
Serves: 2
Preparation and cooking time: 10 minutes
Calories per serving: 365
Freezing: not recommended

Omelettes are the original fast food – and they're so nutritious and tasty. Remind yourself how good they are by cooking some today.

4 medium eggs

4 tablespoons skimmed milk

2 teaspoons butter

200 g tub of low-fat soft cheese

2 tablespoons chopped fresh chives, coriander or parsley

salt and freshly ground black pepper

salad leaves, to serve

1 Beat the eggs and milk together. Season with a little salt and pepper.
2 Heat 1 teaspoon of butter in a small frying pan. Pour in half the egg mixture, and cook over a medium-high heat until the base sets. Using a wooden spatula, push the cooked egg towards the middle of the pan, so that the raw egg flows over the surface, allowing it to set.
3 Spoon half the cheese along the centre of the omelette, letting it melt for a moment or two. Sprinkle with half the chives, coriander or parsley. Fold the omelette over and slide it out on to a warm plate. Keep it in a warm place while you cook the second omelette.
4 Serve the omelettes with the salad leaves.

VARIATIONS Use low-fat soft cheese flavoured with garlic and herbs, if you like.

Add a sliced tomato to each omelette before spooning in the cheese.

For a plain cheese omelette, sprinkle 1 tablespoon grated extra-mature Cheddar over each omelette before folding them over. Points will be 7 per omelette.

You could omit the cheese altogether and just use sliced tomatoes and chopped fresh herbs. Points per serving will be reduced to 4.

Roasted
Mediterranean
Vegetables:
A modern classic,
full of incredible
flavours.

desserts
& cakes

If you're the kind of person who feels a meal just isn't complete without a pudding – then this chapter is for you. The recipes here offer delicious desserts – without going overboard. After all, isn't it nice to think that you don't have to say "no" to Lemon Meringue (page 56), Sherry Trifle (page 55) or Chocolate Mousse (page 58). And there are cakes to enjoy too!

SUMMER PUDDINGS

POINTS	
per recipe: 7	per serving: 3½

Ⓥ *if using vegetarian fromage frais*
Serves: 2
Preparation and cooking time: 10 minutes + several hours standing time
Freezing: recommended
Calories per serving: 190

In these individual summer puddings, the bread is layered in small pudding basins to make them easy to assemble – and they look so attractive when turned out.

75 g (2¾ oz) redcurrants or blackcurrants
75 g (2¾ oz) blueberries
1 tablespoon caster sugar
75 g (2¾ oz) strawberries, sliced
75 g (2¾ oz) raspberries
3 slices of medium-cut white bread

TO SERVE

2 tablespoons very low-fat plain fromage frais
mint leaves

1 Reserve two sprigs of redcurrants or blackcurrants and put the remainder in a medium saucepan with the blueberries and sugar. Heat gently until the juice just begins to run – about 2–3 minutes. Remove from the heat and stir in the strawberries and raspberries. Leave to cool.

2 Use biscuit cutters to stamp out circles from the slices of bread to fit into two individual pudding basins. You will need two 5 cm (2-inch) circles, two 6 cm (2½-inch) circles and two 7.5 cm (2¾-inch) circles.

3 Pop the smallest bread circles in the base of each pudding basin. Using a draining spoon (slotted spoon), divide half the fruit mixture between the basins. Place a medium-sized bread circle on top of each and then spoon in the rest of the fruit, reserving some of the juice. Finish with the largest circles of bread, pressing each down well.

4 Spoon a little remaining fruit juice over the bread and then place clingfilm tightly over. Place a weight on top of each basin. Refrigerate for several hours, or overnight if you prefer.

5 To serve, run a knife around the inside of each basin, and turn the puddings out on to individual plates. Serve each one with a tablespoon of fromage frais and decorate with mint leaves and the reserved fruit sprigs.

TOP TIPS Whizz the leftover bread in a blender or food processor to make breadcrumbs, pack in a polythene bag and refrigerate or freeze to use in another recipe.

Try using defrosted frozen summer berries in this recipe – there's no need for any cooking, as they are already soft.

VARIATION To make a winter version, cook two medium thinly sliced plums and 1 small baking apple with 1 tablespoon of sultanas, a pinch of mixed spice and 1 tablespoon of sugar until soft and pulpy. Cool and then layer with the bread as in step 3. The points per serving will be 4.

Summer Puddings: This delicious, traditional summer treat is only 3½ points.

Chocolate Pudding: Who doesn't love chocolate for dessert?

CHOCOLATE PUDDING

POINTS

per recipe: 24½   per serving: 6

Ⓥ *if using vegetarian crème fraîche*

Serves: 4

Preparation time: 10 minutes + 30 minutes standing time

Cooking time: 40 minutes

Freezing: not recommended

Calories per serving: 355

---

1 teaspoon polyunsaturated margarine

6 thin slices of white bread, crusts removed

300 ml (½ pint) skimmed milk

170 g can of evaporated milk

65 g (2¼ oz) light muscovado sugar

2 tablespoons cocoa powder

1 teaspoon vanilla extract

2 large eggs, beaten

TO SERVE

1 teaspoon cocoa powder, for dusting

4 tablespoons half-fat crème fraîche

---

1 Grease a 1 litre (1¾-pint) baking dish with the margarine. Cut the bread into triangles and layer them in the dish.

2 In a medium saucepan, warm the milk, evaporated milk, sugar, cocoa powder and vanilla extract together, stirring to mix. Do not let the mixture get too hot – you just need to dissolve the sugar and blend in the cocoa powder. Pour in the eggs and whisk the mixture together. Pour this mixture over the bread in the baking dish. Cover and soak for about 30 minutes.

3 Preheat the oven to Gas Mark 4/ 180°C/350°F.

4 Remove the covering from the dish and bake the pudding for 35–40 minutes, until set. Cool for a few minutes, then dust with cocoa and serve with crème fraîche.

PANCAKES WITH LEMON

POINTS

per recipe: 13   per serving: 3

Ⓥ   *Serves: 4*

Preparation time: 5 minutes + optional 30 minutes standing time

Cooking time: 10 minutes

Freezing: recommended

Calories per serving: 225

Pancakes are always a treat. So make them more often!

---

125 g (4½ oz) plain white flour

a pinch of salt

1 large egg

300 ml (½ pint) skimmed milk

2 teaspoons vegetable oil

TO SERVE

1 lemon, sliced into wedges

8 teaspoons caster sugar

---

1 Put the flour, salt, egg and milk in a large mixing bowl with 2 tablespoons of cold water. Whisk the ingredients together to make a thin batter. If you have time, allow the batter to stand for 20–30 minutes.

2 Heat a small heavy-based frying pan and add 2–3 drops of oil for each pancake you make. Spoon in about 2 tablespoons of batter, tilting the pan as the batter is added to swirl it over the base of the pan.

3 When the underside of the pancake is browned, flip it over to cook the other side. Cook eight thin pancakes this way – serve immediately as you cook them, or keep them warm in a low oven until all eight are ready.

4 Serve two pancakes per person, with lemon wedges and a couple of teaspoons of caster sugar.

SHERRY TRIFLE

POINTS

per recipe: 21½   per serving: 3½

Ⓥ   *Serves: 6*

Preparation time: 20 minutes

Freezing: not recommended

Calories per serving: 200

Trifle is such an easy dessert to make, especially when you take a few shortcuts. This low-point version is kind to the waistline!

---

6 trifle sponges, broken in half

410 g can of fruit cocktail in natural juice

4 tablespoons medium sherry

225 g (8 oz) fresh or frozen raspberries, defrosted if frozen

425 g can of low-fat custard

6 tablespoons low-fat aerosol cream

mint leaves, for decoration

---

1 Put the trifle sponges in a glass serving dish. Drain the juice from the canned fruit, mix with the sherry and pour over the sponges. Allow it to soak in for a few moments.

2 Reserve a few raspberries for decoration and mix the rest with the fruit cocktail. Tip this fruit over the soaked sponges, spreading it out evenly.

3 Pour the custard over the fruit. Cover the dish with clingfilm and chill until ready to serve.

4 Serve the trifle, decorated with the aerosol cream, the reserved raspberries and the mint leaves.

VARIATION You can now buy thickened single cream, so you could add a tablespoon of this to each portion instead of using the aerosol type. Points will remain the same.

Little Steamed Puddings: So comforting with custard.

These wonderful mini-sponges are such a treat. The recipe gives some variations on a theme, so choose your favourite!

50 g (1³/₄ oz) polyunsaturated margarine
50 g (1³/₄ oz) caster sugar
2 medium eggs, beaten
1 teaspoon vanilla extract
125 g (4¹/₂ oz) self-raising white flour
6 slices of lemon
12 teaspoons golden syrup
2 2150 g pots of low-fat custard, to serve

1 Use 1 teaspoon of margarine to lightly grease six castle pudding moulds or heatproof teacups. Cream the remaining margarine with the caster sugar until light and fluffy. Gradually beat in the eggs and vanilla extract.

2 Sift in the flour and fold it into the mixture using a metal spoon. Add just enough warm water (about 2 tablespoons) to give a soft, dropping consistency.

3 Put a lemon slice and 2 teaspoons of golden syrup in the base of each mould or teacup, and spoon the sponge mixture on top. Cover with foil or greaseproof paper.

4 Transfer the moulds or teacups to a steamer and steam for about 40 minutes, topping up with boiling water from time to time.

5 Turn out the puddings and serve with the warmed custard.

VARIATIONS Substitute lemon curd, strawberry jam or orange marmalade for the golden syrup, if you prefer. The points remain the same.

To make chocolate syrup puddings, reduce the flour to 100 g (3½ oz) and add 15 g (½ oz) of unsweetened cocoa powder. Sift it into the mixture with the flour in step 2. The points will remain the same.

LITTLE STEAMED PUDDINGS

POINTS

per recipe: 27	per serving: 4¹/₂

Ⓥ Serves: 6

Preparation time: 15 minutes
Cooking time: 40 minutes
Freezing: recommended
Calories per serving: 275

LEMON MERINGUES

POINTS

per recipe: 19¹/₂	per serving: 5

Ⓥ Serves: 4

Preparation time: 10 minutes
Cooking time: 20 minutes
Freezing: not recommended
Calories per serving: 345

Simple and oh-so-tasty, you'll love these little lemon meringues. They're made without pastry to keep the points a little lower.

2 medium eggs, separated
405 g can of skimmed and sweetened condensed milk
finely grated zest and juice of 1 large lemon
25 g (1 oz) caster sugar

1 Preheat the oven to Gas Mark 4/ 180°C/350°F. Stand four ramekin dishes on a baking sheet.

2 Beat the egg yolks and condensed milk together. Stir in the lemon zest and juice. Pour the mixture into the ramekin dishes and bake for 10–15 minutes, until set.

3 In a large, grease-free bowl and using perfectly clean beaters, whisk the egg whites until they hold their shape. Add the sugar gradually, whisking well to give stiff, glossy peaks. Top each ramekin dish with the meringue.

4 Return the ramekins to the oven and bake for about 5–6 minutes until the top of the meringues are golden brown. Serve warm or cold.

VARIATION Use the finely grated zest and juice of two limes instead of the lemon. Add 2–3 drops of green food-colouring to the mixture, to make it look lime green.

MERINGUE FRUIT NESTS

POINTS

per recipe: 18	per serving: 3

Ⓥ Serves: 6

Preparation time: 25 minutes

Cooking time: 2–3 hours

Freezing: not recommended

Calories per serving: 155

The meringues are dried out – rather than baked – in a very low heat oven, so be patient! Fill them with fresh fruits for a delicious treat.

3 egg whites

175 g (6 oz) golden caster sugar

1 medium mango, peeled and sliced

175 g (6 oz) strawberries, sliced

1 kiwi fruit, peeled and sliced

6 tablespoons low-fat aerosol cream

1 Preheat the oven to Gas Mark 1/ 140°C/275°F. Line two baking sheets with non-stick baking parchment.

2 Whisk the egg whites in a grease-free bowl until stiff, gradually whisking in the sugar until the mixture is very glossy and stiff peaks form.

3 Fit a large piping bag with a star nozzle and fill it with the meringue mixture. Pipe three circles on each baking sheet, with a diameter of approximately 9 cm (3½ inches) to form the base of the nests. Pipe another layer around the rim of each circle to form the sides of the nests.

4 Transfer to the oven and bake for 10 minutes, and then reduce the oven temperature to Gas Mark ½/130°C/250°F. Leave them in the oven for 2–3 hours to dry out.

5 Remove the meringues from the oven and let them cool down completely before lifting them off the parchment.

6 Mix together the prepared fruit, and use to fill the meringue nests. Finish off each one with a tablespoon of aerosol cream.

TOP TIP Unfilled meringues will keep for several weeks in an airtight tin.

VARIATION Use your favourite fruit to fill the nests. Raspberries taste delicious just by themselves. Just remember to check the points.

APPLE AND PLUM CHARLOTTES

POINTS

per recipe: 19	per serving: 5

Ⓥ Serves: 4

Preparation time: 15 minutes

Cooking time: 30 minutes

Freezing: recommended

Calories per serving: 265

Try this up-to-date version of a traditional British pudding – you'll love it!

50 g (1³/₄ oz) polyunsaturated margarine, melted

50 g (1³/₄ oz) golden caster sugar

2 medium dessert apples, peeled, cored and sliced thinly

2 plums, stoned and sliced

25 g (1 oz) raisins or sultanas

a pinch of ground mixed spice or cinnamon

3 slices from a thick-cut, large white loaf, crusts removed

2 tablespoons elderflower cordial, made up to 150 ml (¹/₄ pint) with cold water

4 tablespoons plain low-fat yogurt, to serve

1 Preheat the oven to Gas Mark 5/ 190°C/375°F.

2 Melt the margarine in a large saucepan. Use a tiny amount to grease four individual pudding basins or ramekins.

3 Add the sugar, apples, plums, raisins or sultanas and mixed spice or cinnamon to the saucepan. Cut the bread into small cubes and add to the mixture with the diluted elderflower cordial, tossing to combine.

4 Pack the mixture into the prepared dishes. Stand the dishes on a baking sheet. Bake for 25–30 minutes, until golden brown. Cool for a few minutes. Turn them out and serve each pudding with a tablespoon of yogurt.

VARIATION Use 150ml (¹/₄ pint) unsweetened orange juice instead of the elderflower cordial, if you'd rather. The points will be the same.

1 Melt the chocolate in a medium bowl positioned over a saucepan of gently simmering water. Meanwhile, dissolve the cocoa powder and sugar in 3 tablespoons hot water. Remove the bowl of chocolate from the heat and pour in the cocoa mixture, stirring until smooth and blended.

2 Beat the egg yolks and stir into the chocolate mixture.

3 Whip the cream in a chilled bowl until it holds its shape. Keep it cool in the refrigerator.

4 In a grease-free bowl and using perfectly clean beaters, whisk the egg whites until they hold their shape. With a metal spoon, fold them through the chocolate mixture together with the whipped cream. Divide the mixture between four small serving glasses or ramekins.

5 Chill the desserts until ready to serve. Decorate with the raspberries, mint leaves and a dusting of icing sugar.

TOP TIP To prevent a skin from forming on the surface of the chocolate mixture as it cools down, cover with a circle of dampened greaseproof paper.

VARIATION Top the chocolate mousse with a mixture of soft summer fruits, if you prefer – strawberries, raspberries and blueberries would be lovely – and the points would remain the same.

Chocolate Mousse with Raspberries: A scrumptious classic!

CHOCOLATE MOUSSE WITH RASPBERRIES

POINTS

per recipe: 21½   per serving: 5½

Ⓥ Serves: 4

Preparation and cooking time: 25 minutes

Freezing: recommended

Calories per serving: 235

Velvet smooth and very chocolatey – this is a dream dessert!

75 g (2¾ oz) plain chocolate, broken into pieces

1 tablespoon unsweetened cocoa powder

1 tablespoon caster sugar

2 medium eggs, separated (see warning on page 2 regarding raw eggs)

4 tablespoons whipping cream

TO SERVE

100 g (3½ oz) raspberries

mint leaves

1 teaspoon icing sugar

STICKY BANANA TOFFEE PUDDINGS

POINTS

per recipe: 22½	per serving: 5½

ⓥ *Serves: 4*

Preparation time:15 minutes

Cooking time: 30 minutes

Freezing: recommended

Calories per serving: 345

A delicious sticky and filling pudding.

50 g (1³/₄ oz) polyunsaturated margarine

50 g (1³/₄ oz) light muscovado sugar

1 large egg, beaten

1 teaspoon vanilla extract

50 g (1³/₄ oz) self-raising white flour

¹/₂ teaspoon ground ginger

1 medium banana

25 g (1 oz) dates, chopped

1 tablespoon skimmed milk

2 tablespoons golden syrup

2 × 150 g pots of low-fat custard, to serve

1 Preheat the oven to Gas Mark 4/ 180°C/350°C. Use a tiny amount of the margarine to grease four individual pudding basins or ramekin dishes.

2 Cream the remaining margarine and sugar together until light and fluffy. Gradually beat in the egg and then stir in the vanilla extract. Sift in the flour and ground ginger, and fold them in with a large metal spoon.

3 Mash the banana and stir it into the creamed mixture with the dates and milk.

4 Put half a tablespoon of golden syrup in each pudding basin or ramekin. Now spoon an equal amount of the creamed mixture on top and level the surface. Stand the basins or dishes in a roasting pan and pour in enough warm water to come halfway up their sides.

5 Bake for 25–30 minutes until risen and golden. Cool for a few moments while you heat the custard. Run a knife around each pudding and turn out into dishes. Serve at once, with the custard.

TOP TIP If you are eating by yourself, freeze two of the cooked puddings and keep one in the fridge for 2 or 3 days... and eat one today!

VARIATION Use raisins or sultanas instead of the dates. The points will remain the same.

Sticky Banana Toffee Puddings: Intensely satisfying.

APPLE AND BLACKBERRY TARTS

POINTS

per recipe: 18   per serving: 3

Ⓥ *Serves: 6*

Preparation and cooking time:
25 minutes

Freezing: not recommended

Calories per serving: 190

Make these wonderful fruit-filled tarts with filo pastry, brushed with a delicately flavoured olive oil, rather than butter.

---
6 fresh filo pastry sheets

4 tablespoons light or delicately flavoured olive oil

350 g (12 oz) baking apples, peeled, cored and sliced

1 tablespoon lemon juice

---
125 g (4½ oz) blackberries

powdered sweetener, to taste

TO SERVE

4 tablespoons 0% fat Greek yogurt

2 teaspoons icing sugar

mint or blackberry leaves (optional)

---

1 Preheat the oven to Gas Mark 5/ 190°C/375°F.

2 Unfold the filo pastry sheets and cut the pastry into six piles, measuring approximately 10 cm (4 inches) square. Layer these filo squares in six individual tartlet tins, brushing each pastry sheet with a little olive oil. Pack a little crumpled foil in each tartlet tin, and bake for 8–10 minutes until the pastry is golden brown.

3 Meanwhile, cook the apples in a saucepan with the lemon juice and a couple of tablespoons of water until tender – about 5–6 minutes.

Remove from the heat and stir in the blackberries. Cool slightly and then sweeten to taste with the powdered sweetener.

4 Remove the foil from the filo pastry tarts and spoon in the apple and blackberry filling. Top each one with a tablespoon of Greek yogurt or serve it on the side. Sprinkle with icing sugar and serve, decorated with mint or blackberry leaves, if desired.

VARIATION Fill the tarts with soft summer fruits – a mixture of 175 g (6 oz) strawberries, 175 g (6 oz) raspberries and 125 g (4½ oz) blueberries would taste lovely. The points per tart remain the same.

FRUIT CRUMBLE

POINTS

per recipe: 6   per serving: 6

Ⓥ *Serves: 1*

Preparation time:10 minutes

Cooking time: 25–30 minutes

Freezing: recommended

Calories per serving: 355

The crumble topping for this fruity pudding is quickly made by mixing muesli into melted margarine. You then mix in a little grated marzipan.

---
2 plums, stoned and sliced

1 tablespoon light muscovado sugar

2 teaspoons polyunsaturated margarine

2 tablespoons no-sugar muesli

15 g (½ oz) marzipan, grated

TO SERVE

2 tablespoons plain low-fat yogurt

a pinch of ground cinnamon (optional)

---

1 Preheat the oven to Gas Mark 5/ 190°C/375°F.

2 Put the plums in an individual baking dish and scatter half the sugar over them. Bake for 5 minutes while preparing the topping.

3 Melt the margarine in a saucepan, remove from the heat and stir in the muesli, the remaining sugar and the marzipan. Sprinkle the topping over the plums in an even layer.

4 Bake for about 20–25 minutes, until the plums are tender and the topping is crunchy and golden brown.

5 Serve with the yogurt, sprinkled with a little ground cinnamon, if you like.

VARIATIONS This recipe works well with baking apples. Rhubarb could also be used – you may need to add some powdered sweetener, as it can be quite tart.

The marzipan tastes wonderful, but if you don't like it, or you want to reduce the points, simply leave it out and deduct 1 point.

Apple and Blackberry Tarts: A deeply delicious classic tart for only 3 points per serving.

Fruit Scones: Classic baking at its best.

FRUIT SCONES

POINTS	
per recipe: 22½	per serving: 3

Ⓥ Serves: 8

Preparation and cooking time: 20 minutes

Freezing: recommended

Calories per serving: 185

---

low-fat cooking spray

225 g (8 oz) self-raising white flour

pinch of salt

50 g (1¾ oz) polyunsaturated margarine

25 g (1 oz) golden caster sugar

50 g (1¾ oz) sultanas or raisins

1 medium egg

4 tablespoons skimmed milk

---

1 Preheat the oven to Gas Mark 7/ 220°C/425°F. Mist a baking sheet with low-fat cooking spray.

2 Sift the flour and salt into a large mixing bowl. Add the margarine and rub it in with your fingertips until the mixture resembles fine breadcrumbs. Stir in the sugar and sultanas or raisins.

3 Beat the egg and milk together and add just enough to the rubbed-in

For a special treat, serve each scone with a teaspoon of reduced-sugar strawberry jam and a tablespoon of low-fat aerosol cream. This will add 1 point per serving.

mixture to give a soft, but not sticky dough. Knead lightly for a few moments, but avoid over-handling it.

4 On a lightly floured surface roll out the dough so that it is about 2 cm (¾ inch) thick – it's a mistake to roll it out too thinly. Cut into eight rounds using a 5 cm (2-inch) cutter, re-rolling the dough if necessary. Place these rounds on the baking sheet and brush the tops with the remaining egg and milk mixture.

5 Bake for 10–12 minutes until risen and golden brown. Cool on a wire rack for about 10–15 minutes. These scones are at their best when served while still warm.

VARIATION Use chopped ready-to-eat dried apricots or dates instead of the sultanas or raisins. The points will remain the same.

SPONGE CAKE WITH SUMMER BERRIES

POINTS	
per recipe: 20½	per serving: 3½

Ⓥ Serves: 6

Preparation and cooking time: 25 minutes

Freezing: recommended

Calories per serving: 200

A whisked sponge hardly contains any fat, so it's pretty light in points compared to most other cakes.

½ teaspoon vegetable oil

3 large eggs

100 g (3½ oz) golden caster sugar

100 g (3½ oz) plain white flour

2 tablespoons reduced-sugar strawberry conserve

50 g (1¾ oz) fresh strawberries, halved

50 g (1¾ oz) raspberries

50 g (1¾ oz) redcurrants

2 teaspoons icing sugar

mint leaves, to decorate (optional)

---

1 Preheat the oven to Gas Mark 7/ 220°C/425°F. Grease two 18 cm (7-inch) sandwich tins with the oil and line the bases with circles of greaseproof paper.

2 Using a hand-held electric mixer, whisk the eggs and sugar together until very pale and light in texture; this will take about 5 minutes. To check that the mixture is thick enough, lift up the beaters – they should leave a trail for a few seconds.

3 Sift the flour into the mixture and fold it through lightly but thoroughly, using a large metal spoon. Divide the mixture between the prepared tins and level the surface.

4 Bake the cakes in the oven for 8 or 9 minutes until golden brown and springy to the touch. Remove from the oven and turn the cakes out on to a cooling rack. Cover with a damp tea towel and leave them until completely cold.

5 Spread the strawberry conserve on the surface of one sponge and scatter over most of the fruit. Sandwich the two cakes together. Top with the remaining fruit and sprinkle with icing sugar. Decorate with a few mint leaves.

CELEBRATION CAKE

POINTS

per recipe: 150½   per slice: 4

Ⓥ Serves: 36

*Preparation time: 30 minutes + extra
for decorating + 3-4 days soaking time
Cooking time: 2½ hours
Freezing: not recommended
Calories per serving: 250*

Use this fruit-rich recipe when you
need a cake for a celebration –
whether it's for a birthday,
anniversary, wedding or Christmas.
Remember to allow at least three
days before baking to soak all the
dried fruit to make it plump and
juicy, then your cake will have a
moist, mature flavour.

450 g (1 lb) seedless raisins
450 g (1 lb) sultanas
225 g (8 oz) currants
100 g (3½ oz) glacé cherries, halved
150 ml (¼ pint) brandy or dark rum
175 g (6 oz) polyunsaturated margarine
175 g (6 oz) dark muscovado sugar
4 medium eggs, beaten
finely grated zest and juice of 1 small orange
300 g (10½ oz) plain white flour
¼ teaspoon salt
1 heaped teaspoon ground mixed spice

FOR THE ALMOND PASTE

225 g (8 oz) ground almonds
50 g (1¾ oz) caster sugar
50 g (1¾ oz) icing sugar
1 large egg white, lightly beaten
2–3 drops lemon juice
2 teaspoons apricot jam or honey

FOR THE ROYAL ICING

1 medium egg white (see warning on page 2 regarding raw eggs)
225 g (8 oz) icing sugar

1 Three or four days before making
the cake, put the raisins, sultanas,
currants and cherries in a large bowl
and cover with boiling water. Leave
for 10 minutes and then drain really
well. Add the brandy or rum, stir
well and cover. Keep in a cool place
to soak for 3–4 days, stirring once
a day.

2 When ready to make the cake,
grease and line a 20 cm (8-inch)
square cake tin or 23 cm (9-inch)
round tin with double thickness
greaseproof paper. Preheat the oven
to Gas Mark 3/ 170°C/ 325°F.

3 In a very large bowl, beat together
the margarine and sugar until light in
colour and fluffy in texture. Gradually
beat in the eggs and then add the
orange zest and juice. Don't worry if
the mixture curdles slightly.

4 Sift the flour, salt and spice together
and fold into the creamed mixture,
using a large metal spoon. Now
add the soaked, dried fruit mixture,
stirring thoroughly. Turn into the
prepared tin and level the surface.

5 Bake for approximately 2½ hours.
Check after 2 hours, covering the
surface with double-thickness brown
paper to prevent it from getting too
brown. To test if the cake is cooked,
pierce the cake with a fine skewer –
if it comes out clean the cake is
cooked. If not, cook for a little longer.
Cool in the tin. Wrap the cake in
greaseproof paper and then store in
an airtight tin.

TO MAKE THE ALMOND PASTE

1 Mix together the ground almonds,
caster sugar and all but 2 teaspoons
of the icing sugar. Bind it all with
egg white and lemon juice.

2 Dust a worktop with the reserved
icing sugar and then roll out the paste
to a 20 cm (8-inch) square or 23 cm
(9-inch) circle. Brush the surface of
the cake with jam or honey and
cover it with the almond paste.

TO MAKE THE ROYAL ICING

1 Lightly beat the egg white.
Gradually sift in the sugar using a
nylon sieve, beating until the icing
is smooth and glossy. Use it to
decorate the top of the cake.

VARIATIONS If you're not keen on
glacé cherries, substitute ready-to-eat
dried apricots, chopping them
roughly and soaking with the other
dried fruits in step 1. Points will
remain the same per serving.

You could also enjoy the cake
without the almond paste and icing.
This reduces the points per serving
to 3.